Lisa Tilder and Beth Blostein, editors

Design

Contributors

Jane Amidon

Amale Andraos and Dan Wood of WORKac

Arup

Bridget Baines and Eelco Hooftman of Gross.Max

Blaine Brownell

Scott Colman

David Gissen

Peter Hasdell

KieranTimberlake

Anneliese Latz of Latz + Partner

Bruce Mau

François Roche, Stéphanie Lavaux, and Jean Navarro of R&Sie(n)

Studio 804

Robert Sumrell and Kazys Varnelis of AUDC

Cameron Tonkinwise

Stephen Turk

Ecologies

Essays on the
Nature of Design

Princeton Architectural Press | New York

Contents

Preface

A renewed interest in the concept of ecology has recently emerged, driven by a myriad of factors, from the social and political to the technological and aesthetic. The nineteenth-century German biologist Ernst Haeckel defined ecology as "the comprehensive science of the relationship of the organism to the environment," in which each living organism has an ongoing and continual relationship with all elements.[1] As editors of this book, we set out to explore the ways in which "ecological design" operates synergistically across design disciplines, by honing a range of perspectives at multiple scales. By identifying and joining voices concerned about the topic, we attempted to collectively establish a productive environment, an ecosystem if you will. This became the premise of *Design Ecologies*.

The critical essays and design projections collected in *Design Ecologies* grew out of a symposium of the same name, organized by the coeditors, at the Knowlton School of Architecture in January 2006. Given the overwhelming interest in the symposium's positioning, we proposed this book.

Design Ecologies presents a wide range of vantage points and voices, yet is dense with synergetic threads where tangential discussions and commonalities can be traced and mined as one traverses the book. *Design Ecologies* presents a vision that is greater than the sum of its parts; the relationship these contributions have to each other is as vital to this collection as the individual chapters themselves.

Our authors' broad perspectives have helped us achieve a much richer vision than we could have imagined some years ago at the outset of this project. We hope that this will be just one of many timely publications produced by Princeton Architectural Press around this topic.

Lisa Tilder and Beth Blostein
Editors

NOTES
1. Wikipedia, s.v. "Ecology," http://en.wikipedia.org/wiki/Ecology.

Acknowledgments

This book was made possible by the support of many individuals, collaborators, and institutions from around the globe. Through this combination of institutional support, scholarly generosity, and individual commitment, we have been able to sustain the growth of this project through its conception as a two-day gathering, to the extensive and diverse collection of essays that shape *Design Ecologies*.

The symposium, held at the Knowlton School of Architecture (KSA), was funded by the National Endowment for the Arts, the Battelle Endowment for Technology and Human Affairs, and The Ohio State University Office of International Affairs. Additionally, we received generous support from The Ohio State University College of Engineering and The Ohio State University College of the Arts. We would like to extend our thanks to each of our supporters whose complete commitment made this event possible—from the KSA: Interim-Director Jean-Michel Guldmann, Vi Schaaf, Katrin Anacker, and Luke Kautz; and Dean William "Bud" Baeslack III of the College of Engineering.

We express gratitude to our colleagues and others for their positive response to the symposium, and for their encouragement in the further development of this book.

We appreciate the continued support of the National Endowment for the Arts, The Ohio State University College of Engineering, and the Knowlton School of Architecture. We express our gratitude to Ohio State and the Knowlton School for providing an environment that fosters speculative work. We would also like to thank the staff of the KSA for their assistance.

We are particularly grateful to Scott Colman, our assistant editor, whose dedication to this book has been unmatched, and whose insightful, scholarly abilities enriched many of the essays.

We would like to thank those who generously provided feedback about the material in this book, or who contributed to the support of this project in a range of ways, in particular: Stephen Turk, Bart Overly, and Kym and Iain Colman.

And lastly, we would like to thank Princeton Architectural Press, in particular Clare Jacobson and Wendy Fuller, for their excellent advice and commitment to this project. Without their help this book would not have been possible.

Lisa Tilder and Beth Blostein
Columbus, 2008

Design and the Welfare of All Life

Bruce Mau

Let me begin by saying that, in the spirit of embracing new adventures, in 2007 I moved with my family to Chicago. The chance to choose a new home at this stage of my life and career was a direct result of taking the Massive Change project to Chicago. To say we were astounded by the engagement we experienced there would be an understatement. From local school boards right up to the mayor's office, we saw a willingness to truly take on some of the great issues we are facing on our planet and to explore how we can use design methods and practices to tackle these challenges.

For those readers unfamiliar with Massive Change, let me briefly explain a little about its genesis. Massive Change began as an invitation from the Vancouver Art Gallery to produce a project on the future of design. Around the same time, we received an invitation from George Brown College in Toronto to develop a new model for educating designers. Neither institution had any preconceived ideas about what we would design in response; it was complete carte blanche. Our idea was to see how these two open-ended challenges might intersect.

An Entrepreneurial Model of Education

In response, we developed a proposal we called the Institute without Boundaries (IwB). The concept: purpose-driven, entrepreneurial, experience education. You begin by establishing a real-world challenge for students. Instead of lining up fabricated or artificial problems, you drive the experience with genuine consequences. We found the quality of engagement immediately deepens. It becomes purposeful. Students are propelled by a kind of entrepreneurial momentum.

IwB was not an arbitrary exercise. It is our sense that classical design pedagogy is ill equipped to meet the demands of the present. We believe a new model of learning is required. The challenges we face today are not the challenges we faced in prior centuries. The kind of mechanical

FIG. 01 The Urban Gallery, Bruce Mau Design and the Institute without Boundaries, Massive Change Exhibition, Vancouver Art Gallery, Vancouver, British Columbia, Canada, 2004

divisions and discrete orders of knowledge that seemed appropriate in the past no longer apply. Most of the great challenges we now face are cross-disciplinary and require a new species of designer.

We found a text by Buckminster Fuller, where he outlined his view of the new designer as part artist, mechanic inventor, objective economist, and evolutionary strategist.[1] It is a wonderful description of a complex, renaissance individual. The idea that you could develop such a person today is fairly implausible because the necessary depth of knowledge is so great. But we realized we might be able to assemble the qualities Fuller describes through the collective intelligence of a team.

The renaissance team we gathered for the Institute without Boundaries knew only two things at the outset. First, they knew we were about to embark on a journey of unknowns—unknown destinations, unknown protagonists, and unknown outcomes. Second, everyone on the team knew the final manifestation of the journey would be very public. On the very first day, the students were told: "Here's where we are going: in two years time we will be in Vancouver opening a twenty-thousand-square-foot exhibition on the future of design. We have no idea how we're going to do that because we don't know what the future of design looks like and no one else does either."

For me, one of the most moving moments in the experience took place in Vancouver on opening night. During the day, I took the president of the university through the show. She went through the whole exhibit and, at the end of it, turned to me and said, "Last year, your students did Massive Change. I wonder what other students did?" In other words, in two years with eight students, we produced a radio program, a book, an exhibition, an online project, and an educational website. With eight students! That was the reality of Massive Change, and it is the reality we see every day in our work: when you set the bar very high, people go over the bar. In fact, when people are challenged in this entrepreneurial model, it is both surprising and vindicating to see what they can do.

We were extremely fortunate to find, in George Brown College, an institution willing to embrace this level of openness and exploration. We were doubly fortunate that the School of the Art Institute of Chicago agreed to the same thing. The level of commitment is immense and almost counterintuitive. Massive change is challenging for everyone involved—not least for the students who, having worked for years within a model of learning that produces fixed and straightforward results, suddenly find themselves adrift in a sea of possibility.

Positive Outcomes

Very early in the process of Massive Change we developed a position that has become absolutely critical to our work and to the way that we think: we are committed to a critical method that generates positive outcomes. In other words, we are not looking for a critical outcome that says things are all-over bad. Of course, the process of critique contributes to our way of understanding what to do—and the critic plays a huge role in helping us do that—but a designer is ultimately committed to accomplishment, and that's the difference. As far as we're concerned, designers don't have the luxury of inaction or cynicism. Designers have to develop solutions.

It is unfortunate that the term *critical* is readily conflated with a negative perspective, when, in fact, *critical* is value neutral; it is a methodology of analysis that can be used to generate positive outcomes.

This emphasis on positive outcomes was perhaps the greatest challenge for the IwB students, because so much of our culture—our culture of art, design, and architecture—is oriented around the negative. When we began Massive Change, the prevailing mood was discernibly pessimistic. People were very negative about the state of the world and our capacity to solve problems, and we saw this negativity creeping into many neighboring design practices. At the same time, this mood seemed entirely at odds with what we were experiencing in our everyday work and witnessing in our encounters with people around the world. This discrepancy set the hook for me. We asked: why is there such a negative feeling and is it justified? Is it more sensible to be cynical and pessimistic, or is it more intelligent to be optimistic and try to understand what's going on? We set out to explore what was really happening with our capacity to solve global problems.

If there are great challenges in the world—and there clearly are—what are we doing about it?

Are we losing or winning?
Is the world getting worse or better?

The Welfare of All Life

In the initial stages of our research, we found an extraordinary speech by Lester B. Pearson, a former prime minister of Canada. In 1957, Pearson won the Nobel Prize for inventing peacekeeping. In his acceptance lecture, Pearson said: for the first time in history, the world is coming together as one human family. Cultures that have evolved as island ecologies, with their own kind of internal logic, are suddenly being flipped inside out, and must find their place in a larger ecology created by new developments in transportation, communication, and war. He said we now have a global situation; if you want a career of unlimited scope, this is the one, because negotiating this new situation is going to be a major project. He then quoted British historian Arnold Toynbee, who said that, in the long sweep of history, the twentieth century won't be remembered "as an era of political conflicts or technical inventions, but as an age in which human society dared to think of the welfare of the whole human race as a practical objective."[2]

We read these words with an immediate sense of recognition. It described the exact pattern we were seeing. When we looked at designers, across the spectrum and around the world, we found they were using every means at their disposal—whether that capacity was art or science, culture or technique—to improve things for more people.

Yet, I was surprised by the reaction I received from colleagues and friends when I discussed our findings. Our emerging optimism was greeted with disbelief. They said, "You're totally wrong; you couldn't be more wrong." They said, "You're deluding yourself. We should have done it but we failed." They regarded Toynbee's thesis with complete skepticism. On the flipside—and what is truly exciting to me, and one of the best things to have come out of Massive Change—was the reaction I encountered when talking to young people. It was the mirror opposite. Their only reservation was scope.

I said: "Our project is to show design solutions that are addressing the welfare of the whole human race."
And they said: "That's not big enough."
I said: "What do you mean, it's not? It's the 'welfare of the whole human race,' what's bigger than that?"

And they said: "Take out the phrase, 'the whole human race,' and replace it with 'all life.'"

And they were right. Our project is the welfare of all life as a practical objective. That is the project underway, right now, in every corner of the world. That's massive change. And that's why there are millions of organizations working to address all the great challenges we face; connecting capacity to problems; developing entirely new solutions; and really examining not only our own existence and presence on the planet, but how we will fit into this much bigger picture *in perpetuity*. That's the project that lies at the center of discussions of sustainability.

The Reality of Informed Optimism

What we're actually witnessing in global design is so incredibly optimistic, ambitious, and commonsensical. It is so much about forging connections—about reaching across religions, borders, languages, and disciplines—that it is absolutely shocking this is somehow a new image. But it absolutely is. We live in a culture in which the media image is so poundingly negative, so caught up in a closed loop of reporting on crisis, conflict, and violence, that any countervailing examples and ideas are simply not part of the story. What results is a completely skewed portrait of our current circumstance. When faced with relentlessly negative images, it is no wonder people get defensive and become convinced the world is more violent than it has ever been, even if that is simply not the case.

One of the people we met during the course of Massive Change was author Stewart Brand—best known for the *Whole Earth Catalog*. Brand believes perception is self-fulfilling (and here I am paraphrasing): If people are convinced things are bad and getting worse they behave selfishly. They do what is sensible in a crisis; they protect themselves, defend their family, close the borders, gate their communities; they try to take what they can, while they can still get it.

Conversely, Brand believes optimism begets openness: if people understand things are improving—that we are working together to make things better—they will invest in their communities and their businesses, in their culture and education. Enlightened self-interest will make them want to be part of that development.

When I encountered Brand's thesis, I thought it was the most concise description of our present situation I had come across. It is obvious, yet brilliant. Conditioned by an apocalyptic culture, people lose their ability to imagine a future. They become self-interested. The most insidious by-product of this doomsday thinking is apathy—the justification: the damage is already done; we missed our opportunity to act; now all we can do is catalogue the worst of it and watch the consequences unfold.

Well, needless to say, a project that sees the welfare of all life as its practical objective cannot indulge in such a posture of fatalism and passivity. It runs counter to our purpose.

Don't be mistaken; we are not naive about the tasks that lie ahead. We just seek to put our global situation in proper perspective. Early on in our project we said, "If you imagine publishing a mile-thick newspaper called *Reality*, the first quarter inch would be the *New York Times* and it would scare the hell out of you; the rest of the mile would be Massive Change. It would be a chronicle of collaboration, knowledge transfer, and new solutions."

Sustainable Systems

Stewart Brand was just one of several hundred innovators we met in our travels. Another was Edward O. Wilson. In our effort to find out who was setting the agenda and tackling these great challenges, we discovered that Wilson is one of the great life scientists, an unsurpassed thinker and writer. He wrote a book called *Consilience* and another called *The Future of Life*, in which he discusses how the next fifty years are what he terms "the bottleneck."[3] The challenge, as he sees it, is: how do we get most of life through these years? What is so refreshing about Wilson's way of thinking is that he believes the problem can be solved. The resources exist. In his view, we won't have a problem forever. But we will have a problem for the next fifty years, as the global population goes from six billion to nine billion. The goal is to get through this bottleneck period.

One of the quite startling and eye-opening things Wilson said to us was phrased as a warning: if the whole world were to live like the average American, we would need four additional planet Earths. Our first reaction, on hearing this, was to think, "Well, that's the worst news I've heard all

FIG. 02 The Information Gallery, Bruce Mau Design and the Institute without Boundaries, Massive Change Exhibition, Vancouver Art Gallery, Vancouver, British Columbia, Canada, 2004

FIG. 03 The Markets Gallery, Bruce Mau Design and the Institute without Boundaries, Massive Change Exhibition, Vancouver Art Gallery, Vancouver, British Columbia, Canada, 2004

day." But, in fact, it is the best news, because it means we will not simply do what we've been doing. It is not feasible. It is entirely off the table as a possibility. Instead, the question becomes: "Well, then, how *are* we going to do it? How *will* we live with an additional three billion people?" To conceptualize what that means, just envision a globe and imagine it bisected, by a line drawn around its circumference. Now imagine we're going to build everything on one side of the line again. Imagine that North and South America and part of Europe and Africa, will all be built again, because that's exactly what we will need to do. In fact, that's what we are already doing.

Massive Change was organized around what we called "design economies"—the regions of our lives and experience that are being redeveloped and redesigned by these new capacities. We discovered an incredible sense of synchronicity. It is almost as if we had distributed an idea without ever writing it down. For instance, in the economy of movement, where you would expect intransigence when discussing sustainable-mobility issues, there was surprising willingness. The big car companies, the energy companies, the material companies, the tinkerers, the inventors: they all agreed sustainable mobility was the destination. We discovered a kind of revolution, an explosion of innovation and experimentation—investigations of every imaginable sustainable-car format. That level of innovation hasn't been seen since the beginning of the twentieth century. We discovered a surprising consensus of purpose— a shared belief that the task of design is to make new ideas more attractive, more exciting, more compelling than the old, because that is the only way we're going to make this work.

Old Delineations are Extinct

The future of design will be everywhere and involve everything. I realize this is a controversial statement, that it might strike some as a "land grab." I've heard detractors argue, "It's megalomaniacal to think you can design everything." But, in fact, I believe it is the opposite: it is a way of expressing humility, given our past disregard. It is becoming increasingly clear we have to take responsibility for designing things that were left to accident in the past. In other words, we left natural ecologies alone, but we can't afford to do that anymore. We have to take greater responsibility:

FIG. 04 The Wealth and Politics Gallery, Bruce Mau Design and the Institute without Boundaries, Massive Change Exhibition, Vancouver Art Gallery, Vancouver, British Columbia, Canada, 2004

FIG. 05 The Military Gallery, Bruce Mau Design and
the Institute without Boundaries, Massive Change
Exhibition, Vancouver Art Gallery, Vancouver, British
Columbia, Canada, 2004

Future Force Warrior

Natick Soldiers

Natick Soldier Systems Center is designing the soldier of the future. A division of the U.S. Army Soldier Systems Center (SSC), Natick is developing a seven-year, million project called Future Force Warrior (FFW). Part of the Department of Defense's "Future Combat Systems," it will begin implementing in 2006.

The SSC is a DoD installation responsible for "the technology, development and engineering to shield, and increment to our military's food, clothing, shelters, airdrop systems, and soldier support."

Sticky Situation

Krazy Glue

Hydrate or Die

Camelbak

At the Hotter 'n Hell Hundred bicycle race in Texas, temperatures can soar above 100° F, water stops are up to three hours apart, and reaching for a water bottle mounted on the bike frame is potentially dangerous. Preparing for his first race, Michael Eidson drew from his past experience as a paramedic. Eidson attached medical tubing to an I.V. bag, stuffed the bag into a sock, and sewed it onto the back of a t-shirt. One ride with the contraption convinced him to commercialize the idea, which he dubbed the CamelBak. In a clear example of " adoption of Civ Army began the...

design ecologies so they can actually be sustained. We see the evidence of what happens when we don't: over time, we destroy them.

We are still in the habit of regarding the city as a man-made object on a field of nature. What is needed is a radically different idea of the city— one that presents a synthesis of both the man-made and the natural. If you look at a map of the United States and view the areas that have been designated preserved parkland, a bizarre image starts to emerge. You realize these are precarious islands of intelligence in a sea of stupidity. We have to flip that diagram: we need a general condition of intelligence with endangered islands of stupidity. In fact, one of the things we are doing in our own work is moving away from an idea of discrete parkland toward a more holistic and integrated model of ecology.

Design as a Cyclical Process

This is really the new way of thinking about design. It is moving design to a higher level of complexity, so it is no longer about one solution and one problem. We are finally getting past the idea that design is purely visual. In the early twentieth century, artist Marcel Duchamp argued for an art that could be released from the tyranny of the visual, and now design is going through a similar process of liberation. The truth is: the visual cannot begin to encompass the intricate flows, the subterranean processes, the prior histories, and future transformations that shape our practice. For instance, if you take the shape of a drinking glass as the problem, then you're only getting a limited perspective, because considering only the shape of a glass is like looking at a still when the real challenge is the movie. The real challenge is: How does the glass get here? How does the material and energy come to be in this place, provide a certain amount of utility and delight while it is here? What happens when this glass is no longer useful? How does that material and energy get back into the cycle and back to the beginning? The real design is *the cycle*, and the form—the kind of classical idea of design—is just one image in that transformation.[4]

What are the forces generating the problem? Will the solutions have any unwanted ramifications? How can we achieve an outcome that creates the least nonreusable waste?

Sustainable design is a networked ecology. The bar has been set high because the stakes are high. If there is a shared credo, it might be this:

We aspire to imagine, invent, design, and, most importantly, prototype new ideas that are driven by consideration for the welfare of all life. We believe in our capacity to think about problems in the broadest most sustainable way, and to use design as a way of demonstrating to people that these ideas are attractive and, above all, completely realistic and realizable.

NOTES

1. Buckminster Fuller, *Buckminster Fuller: Anthology for the New Millennium*, ed. Thomas T. K. Zung (New York: St. Martin's Griffin, 2002).

2. Bruce Mau, with Jennifer Leonard and the Institute without Boundaries, *Massive Change* (New York: Phaidon, 2004), 15.

3. Edward O. Wilson, *Consilience: The Unity of Knowledge* (New York: Knopf, 1998); Edward O. Wilson, *The Future of Life* (New York: Vintage Books, 2003).

4. William McDonough and Michael Braungart, *Cradle to Cradle* (New York: North Point Press, 2002), 92–117.

Weeding the City of Unsustainable Cooling, or, Many Designs rather than Massive Design

Cameron Tonkinwise

So if we *designed* our way into unsustainability, if the damage
we are doing to the systems that sustain us and most other species flows
from all that we have designed, does this mean that we *have to* design our
way out of it? Is it *only* designing that has the appropriate agency when it
comes to enhancing the sustainability of our societies?[1] Or does this mean
exactly the opposite, that we cannot solve a problem with the same sort of
thinking that caused the problem; that we desperately need new, *other-
than-designing* ways of responding to these sorts of large-scale problems?[2]

This opposition between the first, homeopathic, argument and the
second, dialectical, argument is perhaps too stark. Between them lies
the argument for a different form of designing. If we designed our way
into unsustainability, it was because that designing was always about
designing this or that *thing*. For instance, the creativity and effectiveness
of modern design came from its ability to focus on *this* or *that*, excluding
wider considerations, of longer-term consequences for instance. What
we need, therefore, is designing with a wider remit, a more systemic
designing. We need to take heed of natural ecosystems rather than just
the components of our artificial technocultures; or we need to constantly
take into constant consideration that there are only hybridized systems of
technonature.[3]

But can these more comprehensive scopes come merely from a shift
of mindset, prior to designing, so that it is the same sort of designing that,
in the end, takes place, just now with greater awareness of an increased
number of factors or systems? Or is taking account of a greater quantity
of consequences something that can only be attained by a qualitatively
distinct way of designing? Is the more systemic designing that we perhaps
need, in order to develop more sustainable societies, still a form of designing as we now know it?

Do we need major change *by* design or major change *to* design? If we
need to make changes to how we design, can those changes themselves be

designed? Can we redesign designing?[4] Can we use current modes of design practice to change current modes of practice, or is this sort of bootstrapping utopian? For example, how do those who claim to be employing radically new design practices do it? What about their coming-to-be-a-designer experience granted them access to practices, or ways of changing their practices, that were denied to their peers and predecessors?

Throughout the history of modern design and modern design education, there have been demands for designers to be more systemic. The project of total design was one of the few things shared by the development of modern design on either side of the Atlantic.[5] Postmodernism in design was a reaction against the definitively modernist insistence that designers effect a complete transformation in the world, rupturing all extant modes of material and ideological being every time they design a new building, garment, or communication. In this context, calls for "sustainability by design" revolutions are calls for a return to the unfinished project of modernism.[6]

What might be different this time around is actually implementing such revolutionary programs. Modernism might be characterized as extolling the systematic in design, but the extent to which modern societies are currently unsustainable evidences that such manifestos were merely rationalizations rather than design rationales: a false consciousness that blinded modernist designers to the more limited and prosaic nature of what they were doing. If contemporary "design for sustainability" initiatives are now managing to be systematic in the way modernists could only dream about, what would be evidence of such a claim? What does a more holistic, a more inclusive and foresightful, design practice look like? Or what do the outcomes of such a more systematic designing look like? Many sustainable design advocates, those promoting biomimicry for example, presume that the resulting designs should appear more natural if they are to be more in tune with natural ecosystems. But those designs would still have to interface with, if not wholly restructure, existing technical systems, in which case high levels of artifice become more necessary.

These are not merely aesthetic considerations, but go to the heart of what it means for design to be systematic. Does a systematic design issue remain: Is a more systematic, or systematically designed, social system, only possible as a break from the existing mess, as a *new* system? Or, does being systemic mean having the capacity to transform the existing mess into something more systematically sustainable? To put this more pointedly, is it possible to be systemic and ineffectual? Surely being more comprehensive, more insightful, means having greater agency and being better able to effect change? Yet invariably systems remain abstract, never able to be realized in concrete, everyday situations.[7] As the existentialist philosopher Søren Kierkegaard observed in philosophy: the system builder is like someone who builds a castle, yet lives in the shed next door.[8]

I am asking these questions primarily of myself, because I once believed that we needed massive change, that we needed totally new worldviews and a fundamental design revolution: a revolution *in* design toward a revolution *by* design with mindsets capable of accomplishing a thorough integration of natural and technocultural systems. However, a funny thing happens when you try to be systematic. Far from becoming holistic, you get dispersed, radically, and into myriad incompatible particularities. And there seems to be no systematizing the fragmentation that results from being systematic.[9] In fact, agency seems to depend on *not* resystematizing such a dispersal. But also, being systematic in that way becomes undesirable because you begin to realize not only how much unsustainability has resulted from the doomed pursuit of the systematic, but also how much sustainability, or ways of being worthy of sustainment, persist in the existing mess even so.[10]

In short, I came to realize that I did not want my city to be razed and redesigned from scratch into a perfect system; nor did most others with whom I share my city. This does not mean that I am becoming more conservative or complacent; I still want—and there is surely an ongoing pressing need for them—vast changes to all aspects of contemporary living. It is just that these changes must occur to and with current cities, rather than over and against those cities. This project of radically reforming the cities in which we live, *while* we continue to live in them, will still require great change: not one great once-and-for-all change toward a wholly new city, but instead a great many changes over time. What we need is not a new designing, just more designing, lots more.

New York Cool

Let me explain by walking you through a problem: New York is on the northeast coast of the United States where it is subject to high summer heat and humidity with little nighttime reduction in temperature. However, New York City, along with a few other modern cities, was developed to high levels of density before building-scale cooling systems were developed. As a result, New York has been locked into very energy inefficient and consequently highly ecologically impacting cooling systems. In a world that has trained itself to be less capable of tolerating such summer temperatures, New Yorkers over the last several decades have taken to installing window-box air conditioners. [FIG. 01]

Being a recent arrival, I was dumbstruck by the number of these units hanging out of every building in New York City. These cooling devices are so violently conspicuous, unevenly puncturing facades originally designed to be clean and uniform, because the most prevalent architecture so clearly predates their arrival.

So here is a thoroughly undesigned, yet highly pervasive piece of this iconically modern city. And yet, a naturalist from another planet, without our sense of the artificial, would identify these units as an integral part of the urban ecosystem. They are therefore best considered weeds; a highly successful nonindigenous species. [FIG. 02]

Now these units are significantly inefficient in many complex ways. Window-box air conditioners use more energy per square foot of cooling

FIG. 01 Window-box air conditioners, New York City, 2008

FIG. 02 Ill-fitting window-box units jut from an otherwise uniform facade, New York City, 2008

than larger central air-conditioning units, but can use less net energy when used to cool only occupied spaces rather than the whole, mostly unoccupied, living space. However, it is counterintuitive to shut doors when trying to cool spaces down, except perhaps when sleeping, so window-box air conditioners tend to double as fans, directing air flow between rooms at great energy expense. The efficiency of window-box air conditioners has improved significantly, so that units today are nearly three times more efficient than models from the '70s. However, you would be struck by how many units in New York defy expectations about planned obsolescence in appliances; one of my recent design studios found two out of three were more than ten years old. Units get more inefficient over time without regular maintenance, such as recharging the refrigerant, cleaning filters, and combing dented grills. The energy efficiency of these units is also highly dependent on installation. Without airtight seals around the unit, humid warm air leaks straight back into the room. Units that are exposed to the sun, as is the case for the majority of New York high-rises, spend much of their time cooling themselves. Finally, while window-box air conditioners are intended to be seasonal, inserted in window slots only in the summer months, their size and weight means they end up as fixtures. Over the colder months, they compromise the air-tightness of apartments and offices, even when the slat vents provided in some units are closed (again, a recent survey found less than one in a hundred still in windows over winter are bagged for weatherization). As a result, unused window-box air conditioners continue to function as cooling devices in winter—ironically something that many with overheated New York apartments appreciate.

In addition, there are "multiplier" inefficiencies. Air-conditioning systems remove heat from buildings and blow that heat into surrounding air. Centralized heating, ventilating, and air conditioning (HVAC) systems tend to disperse the heat at roof level, whereas the closer window systems are to the street, the more they blow heat directly onto other apartments and offices. This situation is most apparent in the New York subway system, where the air-conditioning on trains makes the stations unbearably hot. At a larger scale, air-conditioning makes buildings with significant thermal gain more tolerable, sustaining one of the causes of the urban heat island effect. And then of course, the inefficient energy consumption of these systems is, in most cases, increasing the output of greenhouse gas emissions from coal-, oil-, or gas-fired power stations, thereby enhancing global warming.

"Kick the Box"

Here then is a prolific, yet patently unsustainable device. It would clearly be a massive undertaking to rid New York City, let alone the world, of these weeds. Yet, as a fundamental barrier to sustainability in New York, getting rid of them should be at the center of creative change efforts. Let's pose this as a vast and worthy challenge, even if it risks appearing too destructive a brief to many sustainable designers: let's make window-box air conditioners the target of sustained *elimination design*—that is, using all the expertise of design to unmake rather than make, to get rid of some things rather than to make more things.[11]

An initial response to this design brief is to demand that New York City start again, that its buildings, designed without the capacity for natural or low-energy cooling, be demolished and replaced. This facile idea is certainly systematic, but not at all systemic: How and where to move most of the twenty million current residents in the wider New York metropolitan area in order to undertake the reconstruction? How to pay for such works? What is the nature of a replacement building design that delivers low-energy cooling at such densities? This proposal also fails to understand the problem: the embodied energy of such a scale of construction and the associated tranche of greenhouse gas emissions could more than outweigh the benefits of more efficient buildings. In the current situation, it seems prudent to minimize large-scale disruptions to the systems sustaining us. This is why the problem is perhaps better formulated at the scale of air conditioner devices: the displacement of objects rather than entire cityscapes.

Current policy initiatives are focused on getting New Yorkers to upgrade their aging window-box air conditioners to current best-practice energy-efficiency models (that is, heat pump ductless split systems). Consumer education about the power consumption levels and associated energy costs of these units promotes appropriate sizing, correct installation, and effective use.[12] However, the number of old units remaining in New York indicates these strategies are not yet gaining ground.

So what would it take to accomplish the task of quickly removing window-box air conditioners from New York? Where should a designer commence with such a brief?

Perhaps a more in-depth sense of the problem would help. What ecosystems sustain window-box air conditioners and where are the leverage points that the designer might exploit in this species eradication task?

New Ways of Feeling Natural

First of all, a thorough understanding of thermal comfort, not merely its *current* physiological and/or psychological nature, but also its *historical* variability, is needed. Temperatures in the early twentieth century were not significantly different from those of today. So, while historically the wealthier fled New York City in the summer, there were still many people who remained in New York without air-conditioning. These people wore more and heavier weave clothes than we do today and cooked in ways that generated much greater levels of waste heat. But, if they felt uncomfortable, it was not enough to dominate the city's social history records. So, we have become less tolerant of the same thermal conditions; our felt nature has changed.[13]

This points to a crucial aspect of the problem: the manner in which technological devices fuse prosthetically with humans. The air conditioner is one of those technologies with a clear ratchet effect.[14] Experience one somewhere for the first time, say at work, and you feel something wholly new; a channel of cool breeze through an otherwise hot environment is a very artificial phenomenon. If it is desirable, it is a new desire. It is a solution to a problem that was not yet problematic for you.[15] However, as a technology whose function is background comfort as opposed to a tool that enables a specific activity, the air conditioner's success manifests in the absence of other impingements on everyday being; it takes away environmental interruptions, enabling us to maintain "flow."[16] For this reason, its initial conspicuousness is followed by almost immediate withdrawal.[17] The device, jutting ominously out of and into a room, humming noisily, lifting pages, and shaking drapes, becomes rapidly naturalized. Now, rather than notice air-conditioning, its absence is noticed. Homes without it will be intolerable compared to offices with it. We soon become less capable of living without it; we are then monsters who descend into animality when no longer clothed in "coolth."[18] Consequently, the diffusion of air conditioners into the built environment in the second half of the twentieth century occurs relatively rapidly, and then results in an embedded obduracy.[19]

Before they can be removed, air conditioners therefore need to be re-presenced to us. And before we can take advantage of the historical variability in comfort, we need to alienate ourselves from taken-for-granted bodily feelings: our naturalized corporeal expectations of coolness. The eradication of these devices must be driven by, or accompanied by, either reduced expectations of what constitutes comfortable temperatures, or the de-emphasizing of temperature in favor of other aspects of thermal comfort, such as air speed, lower humidity, individual control, etc.[20] Importantly, these other aspects of thermal comfort lend themselves to product innovations with greater energy efficiencies, and these conspicuously innovative products draw attention back to these other aspects of pleasant and productive indoor environments.

Managing Building Service Systems

All of these products would of course have to meet ever-increasing environmental performance standards in terms of manufacture, use, and disposal. However, there would still be a risk that this strategy might remain too close to existing, unsustainably linear consumer-product economies. In general, building-design solutions, whether based on natural ventilation, mechanical systems, or a combination of the two, remain preferable because of the efficiencies of scale involved. Building-scale solutions are also preferable because they lend themselves to business-to-business delivery such as energy-service performance contracting—profiting from the increasingly efficient delivery of a fixed level of "coolth" rather than increasing quantities of electricity.[21]

Crucially, while building ventilation systems, whether mechanical, natural, or mixed-mode, seem to be, by definition, more systematic approaches to the delivery of cooling, they are nevertheless an example of the way systems tend toward dispersal. Natural ventilation systems, for example, depend on carefully designed and operated intakes and releases, and clear flow paths between the two, on the one hand, and carefully designed and operated thermal mass, glazing, and shading on the other. Not only is the operation of these systems dependent on the actions of every single user (opening this window, shading that one), but it also interconnects those users in ways that are difficult to manage (sounds and smells moving with the air flow). The same is true for the building's environs; ideally, cities must first have robust traffic congestion measures to reduce the air and noise pollution that flows into naturally ventilated buildings. In fact, interior ventilation should be designed to take advantage of exterior landscaping.

Mechanical ventilation systems, by contrast, with the less-direct airflow paths that pumps and fans allow, can preserve autonomy for sets of users. However, the energy efficiency of the mechanical system depends on the air-tightness of the building's construction and operation. In turn, airtight buildings are prone to indoor air quality issues, whether from the HVAC system itself, or the off-gassing of furnishings and finishes. So, in addition to the design and implementation of the major retrofits that would be needed to replace window-box air conditioners with more centralized ventilation systems in dense urban contexts, there is the design and implementation of all the related systems: from the maintenance of plantings around the building, to scripting the behavior of building managers and occupants in relation to air flow and indoor temperatures.[22] Being systematic is clearly not simple.

Network Lock-In

There are also the larger systems that rely on the presence of window-box air conditioners, further entrenching their continued presence; these include: the peak-load management of comparatively cheap electricity supplies, the manufacture of air conditioner units, and the contractors and unions who install and service them. In addition, if a successful weeding strategy were implemented, there would be a high volume of waste involved: the ozone-depleting refrigerants of each unit would need to be safely captured, and the metal housings would need to be recycled.

Finally, at least for this quick analysis, there would be the allies that could be gathered to assist this elimination design task: energy companies pursuing least-cost planning through demand management; governmental and nongovernmental agencies pursuing energy independence, the reduction of greenhouse gas emissions and ozone layer-depleting chemicals, the promotion of local skilled labor, indoor air quality, and affordable housing; and architectural heritage organizations. [FIG. 03]

FIG. 03 Permanently installed window unit, New York City, 2008

Urgent challenges—like the elimination of wasteful cooling devices in urban settings—are thus massive undertakings, not amenable to systemic mass-production style solutions. There is no predesign, pan-empathetic mindset that will be able to systematize these situations into problems for which there are large-scale, quickly implementable, and reproducible solutions. Quite the reverse; the fact that this situation comprises lots and lots of problems demands a response employing lots and lots of solutions, simultaneously, but also over time. Each solution will need to be much more mindful of the other problems and solutions around them than modernist proposals ever were. But this mindfulness toward complex interrelations leads not to a systemic holism, but to a plurality of more humble, agile propositions that allow for the evolution of less ecologically harmful ways of keeping cool.[23] We do not need a new, more powerful form of design, but rather just more designing, at many levels and timescales.

There are two consequences to this that I would like to draw out by way of conclusion:

First, the need for sustainable urban-building cooling does not benefit at all from an environmental-ethics sensibility. There are ecosystems that are being damaged by the dominant mode of air-conditioning in New York City, but concern for species extinction is unlikely to motivate the replacement of window-box air conditioners. In fact, in order to negotiate the system we must acknowledge the thorough artificiality of the problem, from the historical variability of human nature, to the monstrosity of people who effectively need air conditioners on their back to be normal in summer, makes the situation impossible to negotiate. The prosthetic nature of something like air-conditioning is not some Hegelian synthesis of nature and technology into an encompassing whole, but instead a messy agglomeration of networks that need, in each case, to be uniquely negotiated—"follow the actants" as Bruno Latour exhorts.[24]

Second, recast as a complex of artificial dependencies, the challenge of cooling urban buildings should be considered less as a problem to be solved and more as a constellation of colliding desires that need to be reconfigured or redirected. The task must not become a biopolitics of bare life: a determination of the minimum atmospheric conditions necessary for existence cast as a requirement for totally rebuilt sustainable cities.[25] Rather, it is a politics of changing wants and needs, in more or less modifiable urban settings. It must be about new desires, not less desire.[26] Deciding how to proceed is an ongoing negotiation around what to preserve, what to destroy, and what to redesign, both in terms of physical devices, structures, and everyday habits. It is for this very reason that we must seek to make reversible moves with which to learn, rather than arrogantly assuming that, if only we could start again, scrapping all that exists, we would finally, and once and for all, get it right. We need many changes, not just massive change.

NOTES

1. John Thackara, *In the Bubble* (Cambridge, MA: MIT Press, 2005).

2. This phrase is invariably attributed to Albert Einstein.

3. Bruno Latour, *We have never been Modern,* trans. Catherine Porter (Cambridge, MA: Harvard University Press, 1993).

4. John Chris Jones, *Designing Designing* (London: Architecture Design and Technology Press, 1991).

5. Tony Fry, *A New Design Philosophy: An Introduction to Defuturing* (Sydney: UNSW Press, 1999), chaps. 3–4.

6. Jürgen Habermas, "Modernity: An Incomplete Project," in *The Anti-Aesthetic: Essays on Postmodern Culture,* ed. Hal Foster (Port Townsend, WA: Bay Press, 1983).

7. Carleton B. Christensen, "What is So Sustainable about Services?" *Design Philosophy Papers,* no. 3–4 (2007).

8. Martin Heidegger, *Schelling's Treatise on the Essence of Human Freedom,* trans. Joan Stambaugh (Athens: Ohio University Press, 1985), 24.

9. Philippe Lacoue-Labarthe and Jean-Luc Nancy, *The Literary Absolute: The Theory of Literature in German Romanticism,* trans. Philip Barnard and Cheryl Lester (Albany: State University of New York Press, 1988).

10. Tony Fry, *Design Futuring: Sustainability, Ethics and New Practice* (Oxford: Berg, 2009).

11. Tony Fry, "Elimination by Design," *Design Philosophy Papers,* no. 4 (2003).

12. New York State Energy Research and Development Authority, "Room Air Conditioners," http://www.getenergysmart. org/EEProducts/HeatingCooling/ RoomAirConditioners.aspx.

13. Heather Chapells and Elizabeth Shove, "Debating the Future of Comfort: Environmental Sustainability, Energy Consumption and the Indoor Environment," *Building Research and Information* 33, no. 1 (2005).

14. Elizabeth Shove, *Comfort, Cleanliness and Convenience: The Social Organization of Normality* (Oxford: Berg, 2003).

15. Terry Winograd and Fernando Flores, *Understanding Computers and Cognition: A New Foundation for Design* (Boston: Addison-Wesley, 1987).

16. Mihaly Csikszentmihalyi, *Finding Flow: The Psychology of Engagement with Everyday Life* (New York: Basic Books, 1998).

17. Graham Harman, *Tool-Being: Heidegger and the Metaphysics of Objects* (London: Open Court, 2002).

18. John Law, ed., *A Sociology of Monsters: Essays on Power, Technology, and Domination* (New York: Routledge, 1991).

19. Marsha E. Ackermann, *Cool Comfort: America's Romance with Air Conditioning* (Washington DC: Smithsonian Institution Press, 2002); Annique Hommels, *Unbuilding Cities: Obduracy in Urban Sociotechnical Change* (Cambridge, MA: MIT Press, 2005).

20. W. Bordass, A. Leaman, and J. Eley, *A Guide to Feedback and Post-Occupancy Evaluation,* (Usable Buildings Trust: 2006), http://www.usablebuildings.co.uk.

21. Walter R. Stahel, *The Performance Economy* (London: Palgrave Macmillan, 2006).

22. Madeline Akrich and Bruno Latour, "A Summary of a Convenient Vocabulary for the Semiotics of Human and Nonhuman Assemblies," in *Shaping Technology / Building Society: Studies in Sociotechnical Change*, ed. Wiebe Bijker and John Law (Cambridge, MA: MIT Press, 1992).

23. See Ezio Manzini, "Systems Capable of Evolving," Sustainable Every Day Project, http://www.sustainable-everyday.net/manzini.

24. Bruno Latour, *Reassembling the Social: An Introduction to Actor-Network-Theory* (Oxford: Oxford University Press, 2007).

25. Giorgio Agamben, *Homo Sacer: Sovereign Power and Bare Life* (Stanford: Stanford University Press, 1998).

26. Allan Stoekl, *Bataille's Peak: Energy, Religion and Postsustainability* (Minneapolis: University of Minnesota Press, 2007).

Ecologies of Access
Access
Lisa Tilder

Examining a number of strategies to popularize environmental-ism in the United States, Damien Cave of the *New York Times* presented a prescient (and humorous) argument for environmental branding in his 2005 article, "It's Not Sexy Being Green (Yet)."[1] Cave's essay, in the Sunday "Fashion and Style" pages, drew upon the expertise of advertising executives, cultural critics, and environmentalists to, in effect, make being green cool. Reflecting on past environmental crises, Cave recalled the 1970s as an era of malaise, symbolized by the cardigan sweater President Jimmy Carter wore while delivering his "Crisis of Confidence" speech (1979), a speech that encouraged the general public to reduce their use of energy.[2] This infamous sweater, once denoting lower thermostats and a dwindling energy supply, seems emblematic some twenty-five years later of a challenging and less prosperous time, synonymous with a "righteous denial of fun" and an unfortunate fashion statement.[3] Ironically, Carter was the first president to bring photovoltaic panels to the White House, a fashionable statement of the time that was promptly negated during the Reagan years when they were disassembled.[4]

That environmentalism might escape its sartorial trappings, Cave recognized the need to resituate the green movement for the twenty-first century. Following a number of experts who advocated a newly branded environmentalism—including Earth Day founder, Denis Hayes, who proposed "the easiest way to make something cool is to get cool people to do it"—Cave suggested environmentalism's spokesperson might need to be a bit sexier than Jimmy Carter, asserting singer Michael Stipe or rapper Mos Def would be better candidates. To this end, Cave advocated the employment of numerous branding strategies, ranging from the use of humor and self-deprecation to irony and satire, even suggesting "conservation needs to become more like a trendy line of sneakers."[5]

So why not draw from a broader rank of artists in this quest for coolness? Bruce Sterling, for instance, sci-fi author and founder of the Viridian

FIG. 01 "Welcome to the Greenhouse," Bruce Sterling edited issue of *Whole Earth* (Summer 2001)

design movement, could lend his skills in satire, as evidenced by a number of Viridian spoofs including the "Welcome to the Greenhouse" issue of *Whole Earth*.[6] [FIG. 01] *COLORS* magazine, built upon the graphic legacy of the late Tibor Kalman, could lend humor and irony to environmentalism as featured in the recent issue, "Welcome to Vörland—Your next sustainable holiday," a parody of a not-so-distant, futuristic tourist resort off the coast of Sweden.[7] [FIG. 02] Drawing from popular culture, comedian Stephen Colbert's "green screen" folly comes to mind, as does bikini-laden celebrity Paris Hilton's satirical energy plan. But perhaps, humor aside, we should consider a figure that makes the case for extreme optimism, a figure who might bring couture to crunchy, someone who can mobilize the masses: designer Bruce Mau.

Massive Change

Bruce Mau established his career as a graphic designer and thinker in the mid-1980s, partly through his creative work with Zone Books. By the late 1990s, Mau had clearly established a reputation as a "visionary" in design circles, most notably as the creative force behind *S,M,L,XL* (1995), a book that positioned the work of Rem Koolhaas and the Office for Metropolitan Architecture (OMA)—and the discourse of architecture in general—as a question of scale.[8] Mau's "Incomplete Manifesto for Growth," published

FIG. 02 "Welcome to Vörland: Your next sustainable holiday," *COLORS* 271 (Summer 2007)

in his monograph *Life Style* (2000), opened an interesting window into design as a critical practice through its forty-three short philosophical mantras.[9] Incompleteness was key; the intentional open-endedness of Mau's set of philosophical incantations was largely the point. Though the variously colored editions of *Life Style* have been touted as "coollectors" items, Mau's "Incomplete Manifesto" advised, in point fourteen, against trying too hard to be sexy: "Don't be cool. Cool is conservative fear dressed in black. Free yourself from limits of this sort."[10] Mau presumably meant to avoid pretension, though he did give permission to copy (point number thirty-five: "Imitate"). But Mau was on to something. His "Incomplete Manifesto" established the philosophical basis for what would later be realized in Massive Change.

Mau's rise to celebrity spokesperson largely resulted from his role in the Massive Change project, produced in conjunction with the Institute without Boundaries. An exhibition commissioned for the Vancouver Art Gallery (2004) that grew into a broad-ranging, pedagogical project, Massive Change was as much a movement as a design project, exploring the potential to improve not just the "world of design," but the "design of the world."[11] The organization of the Massive Change project around the concept of design "economies" was a means to transcend disciplinary limits by exploring the idea of access to systems of exchange.[12] In a cataloglike assembly, innovations across a broad range of networks (Urban, Movement, Information, Energy, Image, Market, Materials, Military, Manufacturing, Life, Wealth, and Politics) were gathered for purposes of cross-pollination. This collection, when assembled, served as a communicative vehicle that became a tool to effect massive change.

A similar idea is evident in the earlier writings of American inventor and futurist R. Buckminster Fuller. In his seminal *Operating Manual for Spaceship Earth* (1969), Fuller argued against intellectual specialization and for synergism. He charted the history of human innovation through knowledge-seeking "Great Pirates" (GPs) who, Fuller believed, prospered because of their "comprehensive propensities."[13] Fuller positioned the exploratory route of GPs through historical systems of knowledge seeking and knowledge control, set within a global network of information access and dissemination. He believed Great Pirates were capable of a panoramic vision of the world, a conclusion he derived from personal experience.

Born cross-eyed, able to see only patterns for the first four years of his life, Fuller came to believe that "if the total scheme of nature required man to be a specialist she would have made him so by having him born with one eye and a microscope attached to it."[14] Fuller thus promoted innovative thinking that paralleled our existence in the "omni-directional space-time," of our "four-dimensional universe."[15]

It turns out Mau stood on the shoulders of others in his visionary quest, not just those of Bucky Fuller but in particular those of Stewart Brand, best known as the founder of the *Whole Earth Catalog*, and for his later work with the Massachusetts Institute of Technology (MIT) Media Lab. Brand conceived of *Whole Earth Catalog*, often described as a precursor to the Internet, as an informational access service. Funded by a family inheritance, and inspired by the insights of Buckminster Fuller, Brand's *Whole Earth Catalog* first took the form of an "Access" truck, a counterculture book-meets-tool-mobile, which Brand drove across the southwest disseminating knowledge and tools to motivated activists engaged in

FIG. 03 "Whole Systems: Buckminster Fuller," one of many access categories featured in *The Last Whole Earth Catalog* (Menlo Park: Portola Institute Inc., 1971)

a culture of environmental individualism sweeping the country in the late 1960s.[16] Inspired by the means of information dissemination Brand saw in the literature of retailer L. L. Bean, Brand's Access Truck evolved into a storefront and distribution center. Here he developed a modestly assembled pamphlet that gradually developed into an oversize volume assembled by a large collaborative team, the classic *Whole Earth Catalog*, printed in various intervals over a period of thirty years.[17]

Brand's catalog honed emerging ideas about appropriate technologies (AT), technologies that demonstrated the environmental, cultural, and social principles of the era while typically promoting low environmental impact, low cost, and low-maintenance tools and methods.[18] The *Whole Earth Catalog* inundated the reader with a vast set of information on a wide range of topics that, in their juxtaposition, formulated a network of design ecologies. *Whole Earth* offered a labyrinth of AT information, distributed under categories, such as Understanding Whole Systems; Land Use; Shelter; Industry; Craft; Community; Nomadics; and Communications and Learning, each divided into a plethora of subtopics. Like Mau's Massive Change, the category Understanding Whole Systems, for example, assembled multiple topics that were loosely organized around concepts of scale, from tools to the Cosmos. So too, within featured reviews and commentary, one found Buckminster Fuller's books *Utopia or Oblivion* and *Operating Manual for Spaceship Earth* alongside reviews of D'Arcy Thompson's *On Growth and Form*, among many others. [FIG. 03]

As *Whole Earth* gained international attention and Stewart Brand's fame escalated, he began to plan for the catalog's inevitable demise. In his introduction to the last issue, Brand and his team of editors issued an obituary, with the following provisions:

> This issue of the CATALOG is the last. We encourage others to
> initiate similar services to fill the vacuum in the economy we
> stumbled into and are stepping out of. We don't see how using our
> name or copy can aid originality, so they're not available, for love or
> money. Ideas we've had and evaluations we've made are free
> for recycling.[19]

FIG. 04 Stewart Brand at the *Whole Earth* wake, on the cover of *Rolling Stone*, July 8, 1971
FIG. 05 "Money," *The Last Whole Earth Catalog* (Menlo Park: Portola Institute Inc., 1971)

Brand began to consider the potential means to support some of the promising "doers" in the AT movement that the catalog served.[20] At an all-night wake for the catalog Brand unexpectedly attempted to give away twenty thousand dollars to partygoers who could determine an appropriate way to spend the funds. *Rolling Stone* reported the following month: "Three years ago Steward Brand decided to start the *Whole Earth Catalog* on $20,000. On June 12th, [1971] 1500 people couldn't decide on anything."[21] [FIG. 04] According to environmental historian Andrew Kirk, part of the difficulty of determining how to gift such a sum was that "the money issue tapped a deep current of unease with Brand and the counterculture."[22] Nevertheless, in *The Last Whole Earth Catalog* Brand acknowledged the role the "money tool" had played in the catalog's success.[23] [FIG. 05]

Shortly after this unsuccessful altruistic event, Brand, along with several colleagues, founded the Point Foundation to disperse the profits from the *Whole Earth Catalog* with the purpose of effecting positive change in the world. Board members were charged with identifying and distributing close to a million dollars in funds to "agents" to pursue worthwhile causes. Although some of the initial projects funded were experimental works like "sex furniture" and "carving a mile-long sign in the desert with a tractor for observation by satellites," the foundation went on to fund forward-thinkers like John and Nancy Todd, whose New Alchemy Institute pioneered "living machine" projects, and Steve Baer, whose alternative energy company, Zomeworks, developed innovative research into solar energy systems developed from the experimental Drop Art constructions of the Drop City community (Albuquerque, New Mexico, 1969). The Point Foundation also funded the establishment of Auroville in south India, where seven hundred individuals relocated from all over the world to form an international community that combined environmental design with alternative technology, converting "monsoon-eroded wastelands into fertile agricultural and grazing lands."[24]

Whole Earth Catalog and the Point Foundation went on to spawn a number of off-shoots, including *Co-Evolution Quarterly*; The Whole Earth 'Lectronic Link (The WELL), which Brand cofounded in 1985, one of the first virtual communities on the World Wide Web; and many others, including a millennial reissue of *Whole Earth Catalog, World Changing: A User's Guide for the 21st Century*, as well as Massive Change.[25]

Buried Treasure

If we are to understand Brand's "access" networks as idea communities, The WELL was one of the first online intellectual communities that sought liberation in what would later emerge as the World Wide Web. Sadly,

FIG. 06 Otto Bettmann (right) at work on *The Bettmann Portable Archive*, New York, New York, ca. 1960
© Bettmann/CORBIS

FIG. 07 Corbis's subterranean Iron Mountain film "preservation" facility, Slippery Rock, Pennsylvania, ca. 2002
© Michael Prince/CORBIS

democratic, participatory network models inspired by the open-source movement have been progressively quashed by hierarchical models (the "money tool"). Take entrepreneur Bill Gates for example. A Harvard drop-out like Buckminster Fuller, and possibly one of the "Great Pirates" of his generation, Gates's efforts to stifle competition (and piracy) have at times negated intellectual synergy to ensure his own autocracy. Through information economies, Gates has built one of the wealthiest empires of our century—in large part by developing closed-source licenses, purchasing and hoarding information for control and profit. In 1989 Bill Gates founded Interactive Home Systems, now named Corbis, to buy the rights to digital images. Corbis owns the world's broadest collections of digitized images, including the renowned Bettmann Archive, an iconic collection of over seventeen million historical images that includes those of Winston Churchill, Albert Einstein, and Marilyn Monroe.[26]

Otto Bettmann, one-time curator of rare books at the State Library in Berlin, smuggled what became the beginnings of the archive out of Nazi Germany in two steamer trunks. In 1966 he published an abbreviated, surreal selection of his holdings in *The Bettmann Portable Archive*, which he described as "a graphic history of almost everything…presented by way of 3,669 illustrations culled from the files of the Bettmann archive… topically arranged and cross-referenced to serve as an idea stimulator and image finder."[27] [FIG. 06] In the introduction to the book—a lexicon of alphabetized associations—Bettmann wrote:

...it has been said that music not performed ceases to exist. The paradox applies to pictures as well. Art not seen loses its meaning....In a picture reference library such as The Bettmann Archive, millions of pictorial items are filed away. What a pity everyone can't see all of them! What a pity they can't all come alive again between the covers of a book or a whole shelf of books....This book then is a ticket to the Archive, an invitation to come in and see.[28]

When Corbis first acquired the Bettmann Archive, it began to digitize the collection at a rate of forty thousand images a month. When it was determined it would take twenty-four years to scan the entire archive, Gates adopted preservation tactics to prevent the collection's eventual decay (and loss of worth). The "original" annals were moved from their longstanding headquarters in New York City to a retrofitted mine facility near Pittsburgh, in rural Pennsylvania.[29] [FIG. 07] Although the public was initially assured access to the archives, the events of September 11, 2001, made public access impossible. The relocation of the archive to cold storage vaults some two hundred feet underground at the Iron Mountain National Underground Storage facility and the incorporation of history as private property raises significant issues with respect to authorship, the work of art, and its mass reproduction. Meanwhile Corbis also has a redundancy plan: the opening of the Sygma Access and Preservation Facility outside Paris is intended to "ensure that imagery can be easily accessed by everyone while preserving collections for future generations."[30] The copyrighting of the world's cultural heritage such as well known works like Da Vinci's *Vitruvian Man* does not only "preserve collections for future generations," it restricts access to historical knowledge, thereby reducing the potential for Leonardos to come.

Just as the ambiguous boundary between preservation and profit poses challenges to cultural heritage, the interface between "access to tools" and the commerce of information can be as fraught as it is tenuous. Perhaps we fare better with Google's search engine to achieve access to information: Google, after all, curates an internet growing by millions of new pages each day. Now much more than a search engine, Google hosts the personal data of its users via Gmail, while Google Earth captures and reconstructs the world's image for their consumption—all for "free."

But while Google provides open access to a wealth of information, it does so through greater and greater loss to individual privacy—a situation where GPs meet GPS. Information economies drive design ecologies, which in some cases can produce unexpected results, as in Google's patent for a wave-generated, off-shore floating data center. While presumably an environmental strategy, this speculative dislocation would position Google's hoard of privacy data beyond the boundaries of nation states within the extraterritorial space traditionally associated with international piracy.[31] Ironically, one of Google's greatest concerns for its data island is piracy, the security of information. Whether Google is hoarding information for corporate or public good, unique design ecologies are certainly being produced through these ambiguous conditions of "access."

The Svalbard Global Seed Vault with its genomic repository is another example, located on the Norwegian island of Spitsbergen in the remote Arctic Svalbard region, about seven hundred miles from the North Pole. The Seed Vault was established to preserve a wide variety of plant seeds from global locations to provide insurance against potential seed loss, in the case of mass extinction.[32] Storage of seeds in the underground Seed Vault is free of charge, as operational costs are paid by Norway and the Global Crop Diversity Trust, whose primary funders include, curiously enough, the Bill & Melinda Gates Foundation. While the preservation of genetic history could be extremely beneficial to mankind, questions of future ownership, cultural rights, and global access lurk uncomfortably beneath the surface.

Benevolent Giants?

In almost prophetic recognition of events to come, Buckminster Fuller decided in 1927 to work always and only for all humanity. He realized that by examining global problems in the context of the whole system— "Spaceship Earth"—he would have the best chance of identifying large-scale trends that would allow him to anticipate the critical needs of humanity.[33] Fuller believed large corporations might unknowingly lay the groundwork for the future success of humanity because of the global freedom they enjoyed. At some distant time in the future, he expected some form of corporate global networks to solve seemingly out-of-control world problems such as pollution, the efficient allocation of resources, and energy requirements. However, before that could occur, corporations would have to shift from profits toward more "comprehensive considerations" that took into account the democratic sharing of global resources and knowledge.[34]

In 1965, the United States government requested Fuller's help with the United States Pavilion at Expo '67, the Montreal world's fair. Fuller proposed construction of a Geoscope that he described as a "giant, 200-foot diameter…miniature earth—the most accurate global representation of our planet ever to be realized."[35] Housed in a gigantic geodesic dome, the Geoscope was to unfold and transform into a computer-controlled Dymaxion Map the size of a football field; Fuller's global mapping system would display global events and all the world's resources updated to a given moment, playing out possible solutions for global resource use.[36] However, government officials felt the display would be more acceptable—that is, less controversial—if it presented the positive attributes of the United States rather than global scenarios that could tarnish its image as a "benevolent global giant."[37] While his Geoscope was rejected for Expo '67 (though his geodesic dome was constructed), Fuller continued his pursuit of synergistic thinking to "make the world work for 100% of humanity, in the shortest possible time, through spontaneous cooperation without ecological offense or disadvantage of anyone," by leading what he called World Game seminars.[38] By "playing the game," students attempted to determine the most effective means of employing the Earth's resources to benefit the most humans.

Some forty years later, in a speech presented at the World Economic Forum, Gates recognized the escalating injustices of world access to resources and challenged companies to engage in "creative capitalism," which he defined as "an approach where governments, businesses, and nonprofits work together to stretch the reach of market forces so that more people can make a profit, or gain recognition, doing work that eases the world's inequities." Gates's speech, "A New Approach to Capitalism in the 21st Century," called for means to address the unequal distribution of resources through systems innovation, in which "market incentives, including profits and recognitions, drive principles to do more for the poor."[39] In an essay in *Time*, Gates described a number of companies, including Gap, Armani, American Express, Dell, Hallmark, and even

Microsoft, that were already implementing the "do good and do well" strategy by participating in Bono's (RED) campaign, selling (RED)-branded products and donating a portion of their profits to fight AIDS. In over a year and a half, (RED) generated close to one hundred million dollars for the Global Fund to Fight AIDS, Tuberculosis, and Malaria.[40]

In 2000, Gates established the Bill & Melinda Gates Foundation, partially funded with monies earned by the Gates' intellectual and creative capital, to address the principal that "every human life has equal worth."[41] Among its many projects, the Gates Foundation is a sponsor of the Nairobi-based Alliance for a Green Revolution in Africa (AGRA), one of the main vehicles for changing African agriculture, by modifying African soil and developing high-quality seeds through a program of seed-related research that the Gates Foundation undertakes with the Rockefeller Foundation.[42]

In many ways, the Gates Foundation's ambitious work might be compared to Stewart Brand's Point Foundation, with goals of transforming profits from commercial ventures to support "appropriate technology" innovation, to do the most possible good with corporate takings. However, author David Rieff points out that private control of capital and the public domain don't necessarily mix easily, noting that British author and activist Raj Patel, who describes "a foundation playing God in Africa," questions whether Gates's involvement strengthens the status quo instead of transforming it. For example, Rieff remarks that Indian environmentalist Vandana Shiva describes the Gates Foundation as the "greatest threat to farmers in the developing world" because of its ties to major agricultural biotechnology corporations like Monsanto and Syngenta. He also recounts environmentalists' concerns with the increasing influence of private aid in government policy: "These days, where Bill Gates goes, so goes government. Every head of every agency… wants a photo-op announcing a joint venture with the megabillionaire."[43]

Apotheosis

In *Massive Change*, Stewart Brand recounted a conversation between himself and Buckminster Fuller about convincing NASA to release an image of the Earth from space. Fuller believed that if people could visualize "Spaceship Earth" they would no longer act as if the Earth was flat and

FIG. 08 First American photograph of the Earth from space, NASA (1968), *The Last Whole Earth Catalog* (Menlo Park: Portola Institute Inc., 1971), cover; Digital map of the internet produced in one day, Barrett Lyon, The Opte Project (2003), *Massive Change* (London: Phaidon Press, 2004), cover

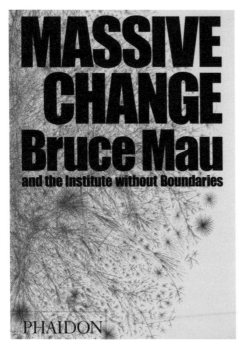

its resources infinite. He helped Brand secure NASA's first release of the image to the public, whereupon it promptly graced the cover of the *Whole Earth Catalog*. At that time, Brand's portrayal of our "Whole Earth" represented what the public could not imagine. Brand recently lamented that Al Gore's desire to use satellite technology to visualize a real-time image of our changing Earth hasn't yet been achieved.[44] If perhaps it has, it is now the territory of Google Earth.

More than forty years later, American entrepreneur Barrett Lyon programmed code for the Opte Project, creating a software program with the capacity to map the internet in one day with a single computer.[45] This graph, which Mau featured on the cover of *Massive Change*, portrays an essential paradigm change: from icon to distributed network. [FIG. 08] After all, Mau's design manifesto was broadcast through a wide range of media, including a traveling exhibit, book, website, radio cast, public appearances, and other offshoots. Maybe all along, looking for an ecocelebrity, or "Green Pirate," falls prone to the same old twentieth-century paradigms. Stewart Brand had it right when he outlined his mission in every catalog:

PURPOSE: We are as gods and might as well get good at it. So far remotely done power and glory—as via government, big business, formal education, church—has succeeded to point where gross defects obscure actual gains. In response to this dilemma and to these gains a realm of intimate, personal power is developing—power of the individual to conduct his own education, find his own inspiration, shape his own environment, and share his adventure with whoever is interested. Tools that aid this process are sought and promoted by the WHOLE EARTH CATALOG.[46]

While the discipline of architecture has a long tradition of patronage, from emperor to church to corporation, the most recognized architects in academia and global practice remain those with roles in empire building. Increasingly we find a trend toward appropriate technologies in architecture, like Cameron Sinclair's call to "design like you give a damn."[47] But can the demise of starchitecture be a possibility within political design structures that reward egocentricity, promote hierarchal control

IMAGE ECONOMIES

Th man nervous sy
environment where se
difference in the surro
mean the difference b
is not surprising that c
forms are practices of
there. So much of life
visible light. Through s
we have reached far b
electromagnetic spect
from radio waves and
radiation and cosmic
glorious complexity, fr
living cells to the vastr
known universe, has b
our visual capacity. Me
of the means for maki
cultural realm continu
As cost approaches ze
production and dissen
new possibilities begir
embrace of the image

FIG. 09 Image Economies
Gallery, Bruce Mau Design
and the Institute without
Boundaries, Massive Change
Exhibition, Vancouver Art
Gallery, Vancouver, British
Columbia, Canada, 2004

networks, and as a result, limit architecture's access to broader audiences? This debate has become increasingly heated during a period of unprecedented growth and development in China, Dubai, Abu Dhabi, and other areas in Asia and the Middle East, and has even drawn comparisons to empires past, including the Nazi Party's employment of architecture as a means of propaganda.[48] The role of image in architecture has long played an important part in transferring cultural values; iconic form increasingly serves to elevate both author and autocratic regime toward celebrity status, while producing sometimes ambiguous messages about the role of architecture in society.

The Olympic Games in Beijing focused attention on this issue, particularly the construction of OMA's headquarters for China's state broadcast authority, CCTV. Koolhaas justified this commission early on by suggesting that China's media censorship might improve by the time the building is completed.[49] Though Koolhaas has mused that market forces have supplanted architectural ideology, this stance might also be considered a means of avoiding difficult questions surrounding architectural ethics. Reporter Robin Pogrebin has examined the stance of a number of architects on this issue. Some, like Daniel Libeskind, have declared public positions against empire building by refusing to work for totalitarian regimes, while architect Thom Mayne has affirmed that his projects in Abu Dhabi, Kazakhstan, Russia, the Middle East, and Indonesia, contribute to an architecture of resistance that helps to shape the way we live. Mayne states that "working under adversarial conditions could be seen as a plus because you're offering alternatives. Still there are situations that make you ask, 'Do I want to be a part of this?'"[50]

There is hope in all of these examples, as resistance to hierarchal power systems itself becomes fashionable again. In "Anti-Starchitecture Chic," writer Philip Nobel considers the "image mongering" phenomenon to be on the decline. He describes starchitecture culture, "characterized by the premature coronation of designers based on flashy forms and blowout press coverage, the infection of schools with the idea of fame as a career objective and…a certain enabling complicity by the leading lights of our critical establishment," as an antiquated (and unfashionable) paradigm. We are, in fact, bored with the celebrity model. Nobel found that students at brand-name schools are rejecting stardom as an aspirational model and are looking for "more grounded ways to practice," with some students dissenting from "image-heavy and form-centric teaching models that Starchitecture has seemingly imposed on many schools." While he acknowledges the economic forces at play, he holds students to ethical considerations, where "the only truly credible course may be to reject the very idea of using yourself as a brand, to work and work well."[51]

If Mau represents design's preeminent brand for a new environmentalism, perhaps his most important contribution is the idea of paradigm change. Building on the work of Stewart Brand through Massive Change positions access, promotes interdisciplinarity and collaboration, and champions open-source information as essential models of innovation for a networked generation. [FIG. 09] So, what kind of pirate is Mau? Though Mau may be a celebrity of sorts, he may hold the unique position of disseminating access to information because of his newfound fame.

The etymological relationships of the words pirate, private, privilege, and price lie just beneath the surface of this discussion. These words share the same Indo-European root, *per*, which has the primary sense: to stand out in front, away from the pack, and therefore to be at risk.[52] Buckminster Fuller's Great Pirates, Gates's "piracy," Google's hoard of privacy, and starchitecture's privilege, share a deep connection, one which reveals the complex interplay between the poles of isolation and exposure. Ultimately, Mau champions an open-source architecture as a strategy for global potential, wherein design is understood as a means of risk taking. With design ecologies we are challenged with, above all else, the problem of freedom to access and synthesize, in order to build upon, our essential cultural heritage. As Brand has demonstrated, only by taking on risk, by both allowing and seizing access to tools, can we open a new world.

NOTES

1. Damien Cave, "Its Not Sexy Being Green (Yet)," *New York Times*, October 2, 2005.

2. Jimmy Carter, "Crisis of Confidence," The Carter Center, http://www.cartercenter.org/news/editorials_speeches/crisis_of_confidence.html.

3. Cave, "Its Not Sexy Being Green (Yet)."

4. Giovanna Borasi and Mirko Zardini, *Sorry, Out of Gas: Architecture's Response to the 1973 Oil Crisis* (Montreal: Canadian Centre for Architecture, 2007), 102.

5. Cave, "Its Not Sexy Being Green (Yet)."

6. Bruce Sterling, ed., *Whole Earth: Access to Tools, Ideas and Practices*, Summer 2001.

7. "Welcome to Vörland—Your next sustainable holiday," *COLORS* 271 (2007).

8. Office for Metropolitan Architecture, Rem Koolhaas, and Bruce Mau, *S,M,L,XL*, ed. Jennifer Sigler (New York: The Monacelli Press, 1995).

9. Bruce Mau, *Life Style*, ed. Kyo Maclear with Bart Testa (London: Phaidon Press, 2000), 88–91.

10. Charles Decker, *Life Style* Editorial Review, Amazon.com, http://www.amazon.com/Life-Style-Bruce-Mau/dp/0714845205/refsr_1_1?ie=UTF8&s=books&qid= 1242953600&sr=8-1; Mau, *Life Style*, 89.

11. Bruce Mau, with Jennifer Leonard and the Institute without Boundaries, *Massive Change* (London: Phaidon Press, 2004), 11.

12. Ibid., 16.

13. R. Buckminster Fuller, *Operating Manual for Spaceship Earth* (New York: Pocket Books, 1970), 9–19.

14. R. Buckminster Fuller, *Utopia or Oblivion: The Prospects for Humanity* (New York: Bantam Books, 1969), 1.

15. Fuller, *Operating Manual for Spaceship Earth*, 120.

16. Andrew G. Kirk, *Counterculture Green: The Whole Earth Catalog and American Environmentalism* (Lawrence, KS: University Press of Kansas, 2007), 48.

17. Stewart Brand, *Whole Earth Catalog* (Menlo Park: Portola Institute, Fall 1968), 2; Kirk, *Counterculture Green*, 1–3.

18. Village Earth, "Appropriate Technology Sourcebook: Introduction," http://www.villageearth.org/pages / Appropriate_Technology/ATSourcebook/Introduction.php.

19. Stewart Brand, *The Last Whole Earth Catalog: access to tools* (Menlo Park: Portola Institute Inc., 1971), 2.

20. Kirk, *Counterculture Green*, 115.

21. Thomas Albright and Charles Perry, "The Last Twelve Hours of the Whole Earth," *Rolling Stone*, July 8, 1971, 1.

22. Kirk, *Counterculture Green*, 117.

23. Stewart Brand, *The Last Whole Earth Catalog*, 438–41.

24. Kirk, *Counterculture Green*, 123–52.

25. The WELL, "Learn About The WELL," The WELL Salon.com community, http://www.well.com/aboutwell.html.

26. Corbis, "Corbis Fact Sheet" (April 2008), Corbis Corporation, http://www.corbis.com/corporate/pressroom/PDF/Corbis_Com_Fact_Sheet.pdf.

27. David Greenstein, introduction to Otto Bettmann, *The Bettmann Portable Archive*, ed. Katherine Bang (New York: Bettmann, 1993), 5.

28. Greenstein, *The Bettmann Portable Archive*, 5.

29. Sarah Boxer, "A Century's Photo History Destined for Life in a Mine," *New York Times*, April 16, 2001.

30. Corbis, "Corbis Fact Sheet."

31. Murad Ahmed, "Google search finds seafaring solution," *Times* (UK), September 15, 2008.

32. The Ministry of Agriculture and Food, "Svalbard Global Seed Vault," Norwegian Government, http://www.regjeringen.no/en/dep/lmd/campain/svalbard-global-seed-vault.html.

33. Buckminster Fuller Institute, "Fuller's Global Research," http://www.bfi.org/our_programs/who_is_buckminster_fuller/fullers_global_research.

34. R. Buckminster Fuller, "The Future of Business" (Lecture series, Lake Tahoe, 1981), 17–21.

35. R. Buckminster Fuller, *Critical Path* (New York: Macmillan, 1981), 171.

36. Lloyd Sieden, *Buckminster Fuller's Universe* (Cambridge, MA: Perseus, 2000), 378.

37. Ibid., 360.

38. Thomas Zung and R. Buckminster Fuller, *Buckminster Fuller: Anthology for the New Millennium* (New York: Macmillan, 2001), 125.

39. Bill Gates, "A New Approach to Capitalism in the 21st Century," World Economic Forum, Davos, Switzerland, January 24, 2008.

40. Bill Gates, "Making Capitalism More Creative," *Time*, July 31, 2008, http://www.time.com/time/business/article/0,8599,1828069,00.html.

41. Bill & Melinda Gates, "Letter from Bill and Melinda Gates," Bill & Melinda Gates Foundation, http://www.gatesfoundation.org/about/Pages/bill-melinda-gates-letter.aspx.

42. David Rieff, "A Green Revolution for Africa?" *New York Times Magazine*, October 12, 2008, 28.

43. Rieff, "A Green Revolution for Africa?" 30–32.

44. Mau, *Massive Change*, 104.

45. Ibid., 89.

46. Brand, *The Last Whole Earth Catalog*, 1.

47. Cameron Sinclair, *Design Like You Give a Damn: Architectural Responses to Humanitarian Crises* (New York: Metropolis Books, 2006).

48. William Menking (founder, the *Architect's Newspaper*), quoted by Robin Pogrebin in "I'm the Designer. My Client's the Autocrat," *New York Times*, June 22, 2008.

49. Pogrebin, "I'm the Designer. My Client's the Autocrat."

50. Ibid.

51. Philip Nobel, "Anti-Starchitecture Chic," *Metropolis Magazine*, June 20, 2007, http://www.metropolismag.com/cda/story.php?artid=2803.

52. Calvert Watkins, ed., *The American Heritage Dictionary of Indo-European Roots* (New York: Houghton Mifflin, 2000), 65–66.

APE
David Gissen

Mechanical, plumbing, electrical, and curtain wall systems constantly convert raw natural matter—solar radiation, convective forces, moisture, and wind—into forms of indoor natural matter—swirls of air, drinkable water, heat, and coolth. Historians and theorists of these processes understand these transformations primarily as enactments of technology and, therefore, as objects within the technological history, theory, and criticism of architecture. But, by constantly affecting the matter of nature, these technological systems can be understood as something else. Using ideas from contemporary geographical theory, we might consider these systems as massive sites for the "production of nature," a term that is used to describe the belief that societies make "nature"—a realm typically understood to be outside human society.

This disciplinary maneuver accomplishes several things: it warps our concepts of what architectural technologies are; it forces us to consider what nature has been and may yet become (particularly in the built context); it enables us to establish linkages between buildings and nature that are more dialectical than mimetic; and, most significant, it signals what nature can become when invested with new architectural concepts. That is, when we understand buildings as *producers of nature*, we unlock something that promises much more than just remaking the chemical and physical metabolisms of nature inside of buildings.

As sites for the production of nature, architectural technologies enact both a material and a discursive process. Technical systems in buildings not only produce consumable matter, such as water and air (what we could call *nature matter*), but they also produce conceptualizations of the natural: ideas of comfort, performance, and health (what we could call *nature concepts*). We might consider the possibilities of the idea of produced nature, examining the ramifications of buildings as sites that metabolize both new concepts and new forms of nature matter. In this sense, our *design ecology* is something that circulates nature matter and nature concepts within an architectural milieu that is itself open to question and analysis. This is both a historical project—involving an examination of the transformation of nature by architectural technological systems from the past—and a synthetic project that might possibly inform new approaches to the production of nature in future buildings. The production of nature idea may be part of a "sustainable" or "green" strategy, or it may involve new, as yet, unknown and unnamed strategies for making nature with architecture.

Although counterintuitive, a growing body of literature within human geography argues all nature is produced; there is no solely "natural" matter outside human reach or impact on the surface of the Earth. From the ozone hole, to melting polar ice, to the genetic mutations of Chernobyl, all nature is laced with human agency and structure. Because human beings can, at an instant, affect all nature anywhere on Earth, the decision to "leave nature be" can also be considered a human production of nature. [FIG. 01] Within human geography, the discourse on the "production of nature" enables us to identify and navigate the interrelations of political economy, social and cultural structure, and their manifestation and reproduction within the "natural." Beginning with the theoretical insights of geographer Neil Smith, and intimately related to the almost precisely contemporaneous work of American posthumanist theorist Donna Haraway and French social theorist Bruno Latour, the analysis of the production of nature foregrounds nature as matter constructed through human action.[1] That is, in contrast to a purely ecological model of nature

FIG. 01 Sadler Lake, Ansel Adams Wilderness, Sierra National Forest, California
© CORBIS

as that which exists outside society, to which society might integrate and aspire, the discourse on the production of nature views nature as chiefly a social production. Once "produced" (versus "given") by society, nature emerges as a site of conjunctions—where bits of nature and ideas are interlaced; as a site of overcoding—where nature is attributed particular powers; and as a central source of debate and strife—where different images of nature stand in conflict. Key social debates emerge determining who produces what type of nature for whom. And the production of nature forces new conditions and situations for complex battles over a right to produced nature. Productions of nature are an endless, but provocative and powerful, cycle. The more "like nature" or "ecological" we imagine we can be, the more intensely (and ironically) we go down the rabbit hole of nature production.

In 2006, the geographers Erik Swyngedouw, Maria Kaika, and Nik Heynen developed a new permutation of this larger discourse they call Urban Political Ecology (UPE), a particularly intriguing approach to examining space and, potentially, architecture. This constellation of concepts further explores the possible relations between society, the idea of the production of nature, and the built environment. Intertwining Smith's concept of natural production with a neo-Marxian concept of "metabolism" and emerging notions of territorialization, the authors of UPE explore how particular forms of urbanization articulate natures of enormous social restraint or an as-yet-unrealized evolutionary nature with potentially utopian capacities.[2] Because this work is focused on the socially dense spaces of cities, the particular social tensions of urbanization are palpably present. These authors claim that specific forms of political economy metabolize the urban nature that adheres to new urban spaces and subjectivities, while simultaneously unhinging, if not outright dismantling, the relations between existing urban subjects and nature.

To understand UPE ideas in an isolated case, briefly consider some of the first, systematic, urban productions of nature in nineteenth- and twentieth-century Parisian street engineering. Through the eighteenth- and nineteenth-century efforts of architects Pierre Patte and Eugene Henard, engineer Jean-Charles Adolphe Alphand, and civic planner Georges Haussmann, the French state ensnared water, gas, trees, stone, and animal and human ablutions into a circulatory vision of an urban

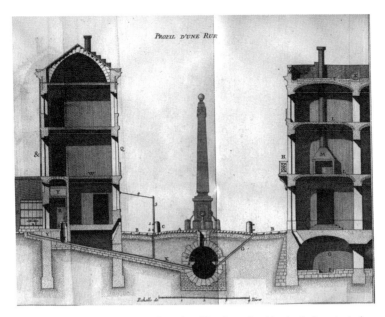

FIG. 02 "Profil d'une Rue," Pierre Patte, from *Memoire sur les objets le plus importants de l'architecture*, 1765

FIG. 03 Anonymous, Rue St. Martin Barricade, ca. 1848 © Hulton-Deutsch Collection/CORBIS

streetscape. This space was designed to circulate both nature matter, "bourgeois" concepts of leisure-nature, and state-capitalist notions of nature (nature furthering real estate investment, among other economic aspects). [FIG. 02] But this vision of state-nature would be reassembled and thrown back in 1848, 1871, and 1968 in the truly revolutionary form of street barricades—vast impromptu assemblages of stone, trees, and urban excrement—that inhibited the official flows of the state-conceived streetscape and unleashed counternetworks that supported various agitational, socionatural ideas. [FIG. 03] The political ecology of the street was multifaceted. For official, nineteenth-century French planners, the street was a circulatory mechanism for nature—"everything to the sewers"—and for mid- to late-nineteenth-century and late-twentieth-century French urban agitators it was something else—"under the street the beach." But both gestures involve powerful concepts of nature production enacted through political concepts. Practitioners of UPE ultimately seek to uncover how such metabolic mixtures of social, political, economic, and aesthetic forces "produce" socionatures that release and ensnare desire and social possibility.[3] In exploring these formations, the practitioners of UPE engage in forms of material and discursive analysis. That is, they explore both the types of nature produced by and for specific social groups and how social and cultural processes further contribute to this natural production process.

Work on UPE only needs to be taken a little further to become an *Architectural Political Ecology* (with the evocative acronym: APE) that can examine and inform the way buildings produce nature as both a material and discursive entity. Just as authors of UPE demonstrate how cities produce nature, architects and analysts of architecture can also uncover the production of nature that occurs within buildings. Buildings, like cities, are dense networks of the natural and the mechanical, the organic and the inorganic, the living and the inert. All of a building's elements contain productions of nature—from steel to carpet. But it is the technological networks of buildings—plumbing, air and heating systems, lighting and electricity—that continually convert raw or semiprocessed natural material into new matter. [FIG. 04] This conversion is both a technical process of mechanical innovation and a process that links technical efforts and concepts to broader social concepts, such as comfort, health,

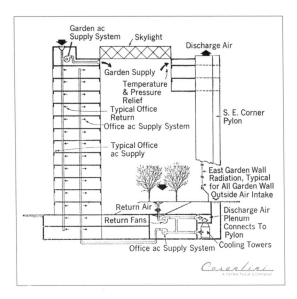

Garden ac Supply System
Skylight
Discharge Air
Garden Supply
Temperature & Pressure Relief
Typical Office Return
Office ac Supply System
Typical Office ac Supply
S. E. Corner Pylon
East Garden Wall Radiation, Typical for All Garden Wall Outside Air Intake
Return Air
Return Fans
Office ac Supply System
Discharge Air Plenum Connects To Pylon
Cooling Towers

FIG. 04 HVAC diagram, Cosentini Associates, Ford Foundation, New York City, 1967 Source: *Ashrae Journal*, June, 1968. Permission courtesy Cosentini

and environment. A building's plumbing system participates in the regional process that converts reservoirs of water into drinkable water, but this process is based as much on the technical achievement of "potability" and "pressure" as it is conceptualizations of "taste." A building's heating, ventilation, and cooling system transforms the physical and chemical properties of air into a property that conditions rooms based on technical parameters that embody contemporary notions of "comfort." A building's skin converts solar energy into heat, or eliminates it through insulation, again in the name of comfort or contemporary notions of openness and transparency. Once located as a technical, cultural, and social form, Architectural Political Ecology could be used either as a tool of analysis or as a tool that informs the invention of new systems or metabolic relations in buildings. As architects search for a politics of form and program, the politics of the architectural production of nature, realized as an Architectural Political Ecology, suggest another avenue for an architecture invested in the New, in all its myriad (and yes, revolutionary) possibilities.

From a historical perspective, we already have the beginnings of a critically informed literature that examines the way technical systems within interiors "produce" forms of nature. Several authors have explored architectural technological systems with a range of interrogatory tools. Among the numerous possible subjects, analyses of mechanical systems offer a particularly rich historical literature focused on buildings as locales for sociotechnical productions of nature. Spanish architect Luis Fernández-Galiano, for example, ties the development of this form of architectural technology to an ontological desire for architecture to harness and engage with energy as a form of social power. Charting and linking Vitruvian narratives of the fiery birth of civilization to the most recent experiments of "solar architects," Fernández-Galiano provides a cautionary tale regarding the positive impact of thermal technologies in architecture. For example, where most technological historians cite the integration of heating into buildings as a major innovation in the development of modern space, Fernández-Galiano explores the development of heat within prisons and schools as an integral aspect of suspicious forms of power within these institutions. He labels the development of thermal maintenance in institutions a form of "panthermicon[ism]," a variant on French philosopher Michel Foucault's famous formulation.[4] Within a historical study of sick building syndrome, the historian of science Michelle Murphy has provided a novel history of the development of heating, ventilating, and air conditioning (HVAC), which explores the mutual production of body image and technology. For Murphy the development of the "comfort zone" within the laboratories of Harvard University replaced the focus on "health" that had underpinned the development of ventilated interiors with an abstracted form of "comfort." The comfort zone effectively mandated the comfort of a man simulating office work in the Harvard laboratories as the standard to be produced throughout American office interiors. For Murphy, contemporary problems with HVAC systems, such as sick building syndrome, are intimately tied to the forms of state science that sought to fix bodies and technologies within the office interior.[5] The authors of the above works provide a more intriguing framework than the typical, "critical-sustainable" historian of architectural technology, the latter interrogate the negative impacts of environmental technology on external nature.

The work of Fernandez-Galiano and Murphy is just the beginning of what might become an engaging analytical project examining the political stakes embodied in the way buildings produce nature. We can continue this work by exploring how the production of an architectural nature constructs an understanding of the larger territory in which this form of production takes place. This would include the various discursive and material productions of engineers, architects, and manufacturers, from technical reports to the often-startling images emerging in contemporary "environmental" designs. Missing in much of the above work, however, is the impact of the architectural production of nature on larger spheres: on cities, territories, and regions. An Architectural Political Ecology might seek to understand how the achievement of indoor comfort impacts an entire city's political economy or the reorientation of a regional population.[6]

An Architectural Political Ecology might also provide the groundwork for the production of new technical systems in buildings. In recent years, numerous architects and engineers, cognizant of the uneven effect of buildings on inhabitants and surrounding territories, have sought to employ a "green" or "sustainable" design approach, oriented toward the *recuperation* of environmental and human health. Aware that discussions of the health of nature are often equated with the health of people, architects explore how building systems might use flows of nature—air, sunlight, warmth, and coolth—to lower green house gas emissions and the volatile compounds within building materials both within and outside architectural structures. This work, by architects such as William McDonough, Nicholas Grimshaw, Norman Foster, Arup, Guy Battle, and Atelier Ten, has been lauded for its positive effects on the "external" nature described earlier, and its "inner" nature counterpart. The significance of this work lies in its understanding of human subjects, whose physical metabolisms intersect with the productions of nature that occur within buildings.[7] [FIG. 05] Such work opens the technological systems of buildings to all manner of new socionatural engagement, but to bring it in line with what we might term an Architectural Political Ecology, we would need to further consider the circulation of concepts in these buildings. The weak point of many sustainable building practices is that they engage the production of architectural nature as a purely material process adjusted through technological mechanisms (air filters, water recovery systems, green roofs, cavity windows, etc.). The systems in these buildings are sophisticated aggregations of technology. Less explored are their aggregations of imagery—of health, ecological "balance," architecturalized nature, and so on. All of these buildings contain representations of

Virginia Museum of Fine Arts Richmond

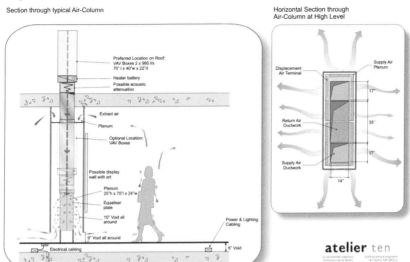

FIG. 05 Air displacement drawings, Atelier Ten, Virginia Museum of Fine Arts, Richmond, Virginia, 2006

these elements, but they are not part of the critical thrust of the work; they are given or reproduced from earlier images of "healthy buildings," from soaring ramps, trees, expanses of glass, or windmills. In many cases, the "zero impact" goal of green buildings reinserts Victorian concepts of a "clean," "hygienic" milieu into contemporary environmental discussions. Thus, in addition to the material aspects of an Architectural Political Ecology that addresses the architectural production of nature, we should also consider the discursive aspects of this process.

Consider the formation of the concept of "comfort," which conveys the material experiences as much as the social factors produced and reproduced in building interiors. The invention of comfort as a social category in the eighteenth century situated an emerging domestic sphere against an emerging industrialized public sphere.[8] The idea of comfort both drives and is driven by material objects that produce comfort. From eighteenth-century fireplaces to contemporary air registers, the desire for comfort informs many of the tactics used in the architectural production of nature. The banishment of smoke from the interior and its release into the space of the city—and the bodies of an unprotected

FIG. 06 Section, R&Sie(n), Dusty Relief Project, Bangkok, Thailand, 2002

citizenry—emerged from an eighteenth-century vision of comfort that excluded smoke and other pollutants from the surfaces of buildings and building interiors. The idea of comfort is inseparable from the emergence of an industrial economy, the class structure tied to that economy, and the possibilities of interior space. Simply put, comfort is one concept that contemporary, sustainable architects try to achieve through recalibrations of building systems, but rarely challenge. What if an Architectural Political Ecology underpinned an approach to building that provided "health" while challenging related notions of comfort? What would such a building look and feel like? How would such a building be realized? [FIG. 06]

Ultimately, the achievement of an Architectural Political Ecology must be seen as a twin project of analysis and productive experimentation. Yet, unlike sustainable design or environmentalist-tinged histories, an Architectural Political Ecology need not be a solely materialist project concerned with an external, far-off nature. Rather, an Architectural Political Ecology would revel in all of the unfamiliar, gross, and thrilling ideas that emerge once nature is understood as a complete fabrication moving through all architectural concepts and realizations. As mentioned earlier, Architectural Political Ecology might inspire historical work on architecture's interaction with nature, but it can go even further, examining the natures that move through the production of architectural and social history itself. For example, archives, historical reconstructions, and museums are concepts and sites bursting with complex political ecologies of their own. Museums maintain very strict environmental guidelines to assist in the acquisition, maintenance, and experience of historical artifacts. This, in many ways, advances a very specific "weather" of historical experience that is only beginning to be understood.[9] Within architectural design, an Architectural Political Ecology might engage with some of the most troubling forms of nature produced by the very act of building. For example, architects might discover a way to counter the skyscraper's strange and poorly understood role in of the expansion of mosquito populations that transmit dengue fever in Jakarta, Indonesia. During construction, the open slab floors of the skyscrapers pool water and their construction drives out the bat populations that traditionally manage the mosquitos that swarm this city. Would a more nuanced skyscraper in Indonesia become the staging ground for some exchange between office labor, insect migrations, and bat sonar? Ultimately, an Architectural Political Ecology demonstrates that buildings are production sites for nature. More significantly, however, an Architectural Political Ecology demonstrates that every, seemingly technical, production of nature within a building is laced with representations. As much as we enjoy using nature to represent that which is outside of society, and as much as we enjoy using technology to discover a terrain seemingly outside culture, we must realize that nature and technology contain an inseparable web-work of human agency. Rather than use architectural technology to return nature to some impossible, prehuman, pristine state, we might consider fully employing the power of the architectural to uncover and produce new forms of nature. These new forms, in turn, might offer us a more socially complex and challenging image of nature, forcing us to reconsider how the nature produced in buildings limits or furthers our social desires.

NOTES

1. See Neil Smith, *Uneven Development: Nature, Capital, and the Production of Space* (London: Blackwell, 1991); Donna J. Haraway, "A Cyborg Manifesto: Science, Technology, and Socialist-Feminism in the Late-Twentieth Century," in *Simians, Cyborgs and Women: The Reinvention of Nature*, ed. Donna J. Haraway (New York: Routledge, 1991), 149–81; William Cronon, *Nature's Metropolis: Chicago and the Great West* (New York: W. W. Norton and Company, 1991).

2. See Nik Heynen, Maria Kaika, and Erik Swyngedouw, eds., *In the Nature of Cities: Urban Political Ecology and the Politics of Urban Metabolism* (London: Routledge, 2006).

3. See Matthew Gandy, *Concrete and Clay: Reworking Nature in New York City* (Cambridge, MA: MIT Press, 2002); Eric Swyngedouw, "Circulating Waters, Circulating Moneys, Contested Natures," in *Patterned Ground: Entanglements of Nature and Culture*, ed. Stephan Harrison, Steve Pile, and Nigel Thrift (London: Reaktion, 2004); Maria Kaika, *City of Flows: Modernity, Nature, and the City* (London: Routledge, 2005).

4. See Luis Fernández-Galiano, *Fire and Memory: On Architecture and Energy* (Cambridge, MA: MIT Press, 2000).

5. See Michelle Murphy, *Sick Building Syndrome and the Problem of Uncertainty: Environmental Politics, Technoscience, and Women Workers* (Durham: Duke University Press, 2006).

6. See David Gissen, "Exhaust and Territorialisation at the Washington Bridge Apartments, New York City, 1963–1973," *Journal of Architecture* 12, no. 4 (September 2007): 449–61.

7. See David Gissen, ed., *Big and Green: Towards Sustainable Architecture in the Twenty-First Century* (New York: Princeton Architectural Press, 2003).

8. See John E. Crowley, *The Invention of Comfort* (Baltimore: Johns Hopkins University Press, 2001).

9. For APE historical work see David Gissen, "The Architectural Production of Nature, Dendur/New York" *Grey Room*, 34 (Winter 2009): 58–79; David Gissen "Energy Histories" in *Energies: New Material Boundaries, AD*, ed. Sean Lally (April 2009); and David Gissen, "HTC Experiments," http://htcexperiments.org.

I'mlostinParis

François Roche,
Stéphanie Lavaux,
and Jean Navarro
of R&Sie(n)

It's the story of an urban witch, living behind a Rear Window, a private laboratory designed as a Duck Blind cabana. An alchemist, she feeds the plants drop by drop; a hydroponic system—rainwater mixed with bacterial preparations disseminated through three hundred light-refracting glass beakers to the surfaces of twelve hundred ferns ("dinosaurs" of the Devonian period, domesticated for the regressive French period).

The neighborhood is both attracted by the green aspect and repulsed by the potion and the process. Eros is not so far from Thanatos....

FIGS. 01-05 l'mlostinParis, R&Sie(n), France, 2008

Green Screens: Modernism's Secret Garden

Robert Sumrell
and Kazys Varnelis
of AUDC

Having exploited the planet to feed our ravenous consumerist desires, we now face impending ecological collapse. Rising temperatures, melting ice fields, soaring food prices, massive storms, and drowning polar bears appear in the headlines daily, demanding immediate action as our everyday lives are threatened. Advocates of green design urge architects to appeal to the ecological consciousness of the consumer by mitigating the environmental effects of the construction and inhabitation of the built domain.

This is not the first time architects have been faced with these issues. In the 1960s and '70s, increasing pollution, dwindling resources, and environmental degradation appeared to imperil the Earth. Books like Rachel Carson's *Silent Spring* (1962), Paul R. Ehrlich's *The Population Bomb* (1968), and the Club of Rome's *The Limits to Growth* (1972) argued humanity's lack of concern for the environment had produced a dangerous imbalance in the ecosystem. Artists such as Robert Smithson and Joseph Beuys drew attention to our alienated relationship to the environment, questioning the distinction between the artificial and the natural and the Judeo-Christian advocacy of man's role as the steward of his environment. Theorists and architecture critics also reacted with concern, in texts such as Peter Blake's *God's Own Junkyard: The Planned Deterioration of America's Landscape* (1964) and Nathaniel Owings's *The American Aesthetic* (1969).

But modern design—and even architecture itself—had become thoroughly associated with Fordist enterprise and its faith in technology and production, a position that an increasingly environmentally conscious public blamed for the destruction of the environment. Compounding this loss of faith, a protracted recession made new building difficult. In response, architects of the early 1970s turned away from new construction and instead sought to recontextualize existing buildings, challenging modernism's advocacy of the tabula rasa and condemning its reliance on the ground-up replacement of existing structures. Understanding the rapid spread of this first green movement helps us better come to terms with our present situation.

The roots of the economic contraction of the early 1970s lay in the transition from a production-based Fordist economy to a consumption-based post-Fordist economy. Thus, it should be no surprise that, instead of the office, factory, or single-family house (seen as a place for the production of children and the nuclear family), architects increasingly focused on sites of consumption.

At this point the first wave of baby boomers had finished college and began entering the work force in large numbers. Childless and unmarried, young people (an increasing percentage of whom were gay) were eager to find appropriate venues for socializing, befitting their informal nature. In response, designers developed a new, early form of green architecture, the "fern bar."

The first fern bar was Henry Africa's, founded in 1970, in San Francisco. Virtually all at once, Henry Africa's defined the fern bar now familiar to us: exposed brick walls (referring to the popular loft renovations of the time, signifying authenticity while evoking an obsolete world of manufacture now turned charmingly idle), chalk boards with the day's menu (suggesting fresh-from-the-farm ingredients but also symbols of informality and flexibility recalling the innocent days of childhood), and Victoriana such as lamps and old signs (a reference to the popular Victorian, thrift-store chic of the day), and a wealth of potted plants.

The introduction of plants at fern bars was crucial. Already, at the Four Seasons restaurant in the Seagram Building, potted trees in the dining rooms tempered the severity of the Miesian idiom. Menus changed every season, in keeping with the restaurant's name, and so did the trees, allowing restaurateur Joe Baum to create an impression of freshness and to recall the eternal rhythms of nature. Aiding this, the bronze curtains of textile designer Marie Richards waved gently above the restaurant's forced air ducts, giving a faster rhythm to the space, at once enlivening and softening.[1] The potted plants spread throughout fern bars like Henry Africa's, frequently placed in hanging baskets (often wicker or woven), were even more effective; they were informal elements that livened the space and soon became symbols in themselves.

Into the 1970s, bars were masculine places, either clubby lounges (the Four Seasons falls in this category) or neighborhood pubs, aggressively masculine institutions in which women did not feel welcome. In contrast, a fern in a window came to suggest that the bar welcomed single women seeking men, married men, and homosexuals (during the 1970s, more straight, single, and married men began experimenting with bisexuality and homosexuality).

Plants allowed fern bars to play a subtle game with the street. On the one hand, unlike older bars that tried to shut off the street to simulate the night, fern bars generally had large windows that let in daylight and allowed individuals to see in, to ensure the scene was acceptable for them. In many ways, the fern bar served as an extension of the street, containing its hustle, sexuality, and drug culture.[2] On the other hand, by obscuring patrons from view, plants protected the identities of individuals. Ferns announced the bar as an informal place of sexual encounter for a new public (the Me generation) that openly sought self-gratification.

Generally serving food, fern bars gave women who wanted to get drunk or meet men the alibi that they were just going out for dinner. The early 1970s was a crucial social moment, as women began to feel more comfortable going out in groups, or on their own. With easy access to the birth control pill and, after 1973, abortion as well, women were able to enjoy sex that appeared, at least initially, to be without consequences. The image of female sexuality as plantlike was common at the time. The flowerlike appearance of the vulva, peering through the wild tangle of pubic hair (frequently called a bush), coupled with the idea of the woman as fertile (even if paradoxically, birth control measures counteracted this fertility) gave rise to this idea of plantlike female erogenous zones. This connection was often direct and literal, as in the paintings of Georgia O'Keefe popular at the time, or the artwork of Judy Chicago. In 1973, feminist author Nancy Friday published a collection of women's sexual fantasies, *My Secret Garden*, derived from taped and written interviews.[3] If intended to affirm women's sexuality, *My Secret Garden* also explored its darker side, including masochism, bestiality, prostitution, and interracial rape (the narrator in *My Secret Garden* describes rape as the only "safe" form of interracial sex for white women). The secret garden was a place in which women could submit to their darkest desires.

This dark side of the fern bar was apparent in its historical referent, the Victorian boudoir. Tiffany lamps were commonly employed in fern bars as was Victorian or art nouveau script, itself florid and sexually suggestive. Houseplants—and ferns in particular—had been popular in Victorian interiors as symbols of propriety and morality, even if such places were, at least in their 1970s recuperation, filled with forbidden desire. By the late 1960s, the Victorian era, long characterized as repressive, was being recovered as a period in which, underneath surface repression, a wild sexuality flourished. Women of the 1970s celebrated their sexual independence by pointing not to the repressed and dependent Victorian housewife, but rather to the sexually fulfilled and independent prostitute (such as the character of Constance Miller, in film director Robert Altman's 1971 Victorian-themed Western *McCabe and Mrs. Miller*).

But the casual sexual encounters of the fern bar could be dangerous. The most famous such incident occurred at W. M. Tweeds, an Upper West Side Manhattan fern bar named after Boss (William Marcy) Tweed, a notoriously corrupt figure in New York City's nineteenth-century "Tammany Hall" political machine. Here, a schoolteacher named Roseann Quinn met men she took home for casual sex that, according to her neighbors, steadily escalated in violence. On New Year's Eve, 1972, Quinn met John Wayne Wilson, who would murder her that evening (according to Wilson, she begged to be murdered) and her story would become the inspiration for the 1975 novel and 1977 movie *Looking for Mr. Goodbar*.[4] After the murder, W. M. Tweeds would be renamed the All State Café and serve as an inspiration for the television series *Cheers* (a show encapsulated in the catchphrase of its theme song—"Where everybody knows your name"—suggesting a place of protection and safety, where casual sexual encounters were limited to a circle of friends).[5]

As the first generation of baby boomers married, reproduced, and moved to the suburbs, the fern bar stopped being a place of sexual encounter. Not having experienced the OPEC energy crisis and Vietnam firsthand, tired of environmental and political consciousness, a new generation turned instead to the disco for its glamorous, fashion-oriented scene and more openly sexual connotations. The fern bar would be desexualized, absorbed by chains like Bennigan's and Chili's, to which boomers could go for high-calorie family dinners and powerful drinks with friends from work, before driving home for an evening in front of the television.

In its classic form, the fern bar provides an alibi. It promises safety; a place in which women and men can coexist without threat. But it is really not safe, nor is it supposed to be. The fern acts as a mediator of the impersonality of modern life; an element that allows us to achieve the impersonality we really want but pretend otherwise. As something between the living and an object, the fern makes it possible for us to feel comfortable becoming (sexual) objects in the eyes of others.

As an early moment of ecological architecture, the fern bar makes the moral duplicity of green design apparent. Shut off from the light, their leaves covered in dust, grease, and eventually disease, the plants in a fern bar swiftly died. But in giving themselves up, the ferns allowed their patrons to do what they really wanted, to seek self-gratification. The green movement today allows us this too. Living in green homes, working in LEED-certified offices, and eating organic food allows us to pretend we are saving the world, when, in reality, we are only ratcheting up consumption in an unprecedented drunken frenzy. Green design makes the world our fern bar. While we saddle up and enjoy the fantasy, the tab stays open.

NOTES

1. See Phyllis Lambert, "Stimmung at Seagram: Philip Johnson Counters Mies van der Rohe," *Grey Room*, 20 (2005): 38–59.

2. John Irwin, *Scenes* (Beverly Hills: Sage Publications, 1977), 36.

3. Nancy Friday, *My Secret Garden: Women's Sexual Fantasies* (New York: Trident Press, 1973).

4. Judith Rossner, *Looking for Mr. Goodbar* (New York: Simon and Schuster, 1975).

5. Winter Miller, "One More Storied Bar Falls Victim to Rising Rents," *New York Times,* October 25, 2007.

Pneuma:
An Indeterminate
Architecture,
or, Toward a
Soft and Weedy
Architecture
Peter Hasdell

Designed Ecologies, Second Nature

If architecture can be understood to connect the outside, natural world at large with the regulated, controlled, and inhabited inner life at a specific location, then architecture's response to its milieu—its siting, orientation, and location—implies an "appropriateness" within a locale, context, or region. The history of a contextual architecture exemplified by genus loci (spirit of place) could be said to have strongly influenced the development of ecological approaches in design, whether by passive principles—that lead to particular ways to orient and mass a building—or through concepts such as the ecological footprint of buildings and cities.[1] Now, as LEED ratings encourage the use of local materials, and as building authorities begin to require embodied energy and life cycle calculations, these contextual issues again come to the fore. Through these and other frameworks of sustainability, the field of architecture and ecological design has expanded and extended the idea of the building context. Coupled with this is the increasing sophistication of sustainable building technologies. Ecological design has become a complex operation. As architectural practice has moved toward a consideration of its extended milieu, its parallel, diabolical oppositions—the over use of resources and the promotion of excess—have just as surely severed these sutures. As such, notions for a general concept of ecology and ecological design—a single "best fit" model—leave much to be desired.

By contrast, a possible framework for reconceptualizing the design of ecologies as a raw, open-ended, open-sourced, and nonprescriptive research-based practice is outlined below as Pneuma. [FIG. 01] As a point of departure, this practice comprehends architecture as a mediating entity (a medium) that regulates flows and balances in an ecological field. Pneuma terms this approach as "second nature," a second order condition that encompasses both natural and synthetic environmental principles. In this schema, a building's walls, roofs, and floors become filters and registers

FIG. 01 Shadow projections, Peter Hasdell and Patrick Harrop, Pneus, Monopoli Gallery, Montreal, Quebec, Canada, 2008

of differences; thus the passive elements across which we can measure quantitative and register qualitative change become indicators of environmental differences between "nature" and a culturally determined internal environment. Architecture can be situated at this mediating juncture between a natural order and a synthetic, man-made order. And, in these terms, it can be reinterpreted as variable, responsive, and mutable in relation to its milieu. Further, an architecture that is reactive, responsive, and adaptive in relationship to its milieu becomes ever more biological in operation and, perhaps, ever more approximating a life-form. Broader issues, such as the interdependency of systems and biomimetic principles that derive or engineer particular design applications from the study of an organism, are factors that, when compared to natural systems, are still in their infancy in architecture. In a "second nature" approach, ecological design considerations of energy consumption, or embodied energy, would begin to approach the concepts of food webs and nutrient flows found in a biological ecosystem. This implies a number of necessary shifts: privileging morphologies over forms, genotypes over typologies, and cell walls and membranes over traditionally conceived walls. [FIG. 02]

In parallel to advances in ecological design, the digital realm has proliferated, becoming ubiquitous as our prosthetic extension to the world. During its first half-century, the digital realm has generally been a top-down system. The potential of the digital—as complex autonomous systems that behave in ways more akin to living things in the natural world—is only now beginning to be actualized. In *Out of Control*, Kevin Kelly argues the need for a more autonomous, swarmlike order of computing. He writes: "[A]s we unleash living forces into our created machines, we lose control of them. They acquire wildness.... "[2] As the digital realm evolves—new forms of distributed computing are employing cognitive, sensory, and interactive abilities, such as inbuilt feedback mechanisms and predictive and collective behaviors—the overall characteristics of our digital systems more closely approximate, and are able to interact with, human and natural systems. American postmodern critic N. Katherine Hayles points out that essential decision processes in complex systems have developed in ways that now require both human and computer input. To situate this juncture as an emerging condition, Hayles explains that "the development of distributed cognitive environments in which

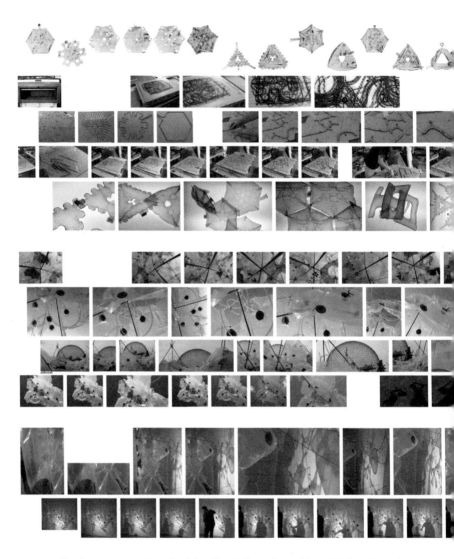

FIG. 02 Development process, Peter Hasdell and Patrick Harrop, Pneus, Monopoli Gallery, Montreal, Quebec, Canada, 2008

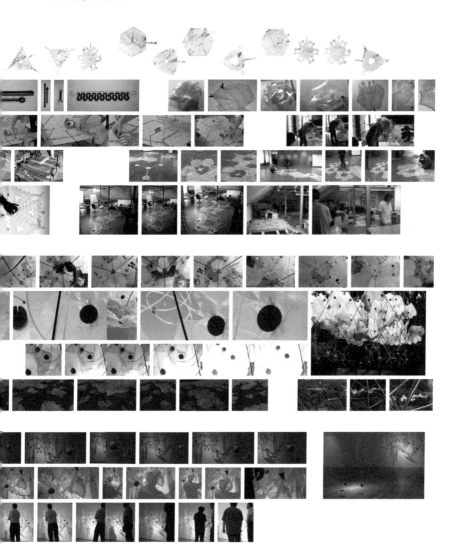

humans and computers interact in hundreds of ways daily, often unob-
trusively" has transformed data and information into a flow independent
of its material base, creating the possibility for a new condition that links
data and computer networks with human networks. Hayles speaks of this
condition, "not as a dichotomy between the real and virtual but rather as
space in which the natural and the artificial are increasingly entwined,"
foreseeing the growth of what social theorist Bruno Latour calls "quasi-
objects": a multitude of hybrid objects produced by a collaboration
between nature and culture.[3] The 2005 United Nations International
Telecommunications Union report, "The Internet of Things," supports
Latour's point of view, outlining an increasing degree of embedded computing within our everyday environments, a proliferation of computing
to the extent that interactions between multiple embedded parts may, in
the near future, outnumber actual human-computer interactions.[4] This
ubiquitous distributed computing will impact our notion of the environment, and the interaction between entities (artificial or natural) within
those environments.

This conceptually is related to the field of cybernetics, or, more
precisely, "new" or second-order cybernetics. Cybernetics, as originally
developed by American mathematician Norbert Wiener in the 1950s, was
concerned with the regulation, self-organization, and governance of systems natural and synthetic, social and organizational. The self-regulation
in cybernetic systems is significant as it necessarily includes feedback
systems and, by implication, sensory capabilities to effect this regulation.
Other proponents of cybernetics included the inimitable British psycholo-
gist Gordon Pask, for many years a senior lecturer at the Architectural
Association. Pask collaborated with British architect Cedric Price on
many of his innovative and cybernetics-derived projects. Pask's approach,
while cognizant of the fields of computing and electronics, chose to focus
instead on human interaction through his "Conversation Theory" (as
opposed to pure data or information). Despite its broad-ranging premise, in its initial synthesis, cybernetics was reductively applied to limited,
technocratic attributes of information, and computing and machine
control, connoting cyborgs and the autonomous control (self-regulation)
of information systems. In its rediscovery and redefinition in the 1970s,
cybernetics took on a more biological role through proponents such as

Chilean biologists Francisco Varela and Humberto Maturana who defined the term *autopoiesis* as a conceptual mechanism:

> An autopoietic machine is a machine organized (defined as a unity) as
> a network of processes of production (transformation and destruction)
> of components which: (i) through their interactions and transforma-
> tions continuously regenerate and realize the network of processes
> (relations) that produced them; and (ii) constitute it (the machine) as a
> concrete unity in space in which they (the components) exist by specify-
> ing the topological domain of its realization as such a network.[5]

Autopoiesis or "self-creation" describes the cybernetic or regulating systems that give rise to and maintain biological cells and living systems. Within this concept, the flow of energy and matter (molecules) is considered integral to the overall autonomy of the system, as is the system's processes of cognition. Because Maturana and Varela's cybernetic theory of autopoiesis refers to closed or bounded biological systems—in other words, an organism's capacity to make and maintain itself—it allows innumerable parallels to a more biological definition of ecology. [FIG. 03]

More specifically, as computing develops, employing cognitive, sensory, and interactive attributes as inbuilt feedback mechanisms, the overall behavioral characteristics of a digital system are increasingly able to engage the complex dynamics of both human and natural systems. Emerging fusions of the natural and the digital are only just beginning to engage issues of biomimesis, emergent properties, environmental responsiveness, autonomous behaviors, and artificial ecosystems, in which a truly hybrid natural and digital environment—a "second nature"—arises. Second nature, as it is commonly understood, is an acquired behavior practiced long enough to become innate, or "natural." It is also a learned physical and emotional response that modifies our relation to the world and allows us, in this case, to access both the natural and the digital.[6] Emerging fields of research on morphological, digital, and media ecologies are beginning to extend the concept of ecology beyond the natural biotope. At its base, this research suggests ecology is not the exclusive domain of the environmentalist. A further implication is that different types of ecologies could share commonalities and relationships

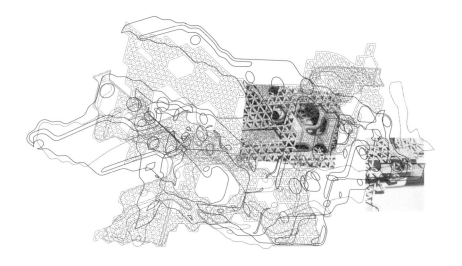

FIG. 03 Model, Peter Hasdell and Patrick Harrop, Pneuma Assemblage, Pneuma Device, Joyce Yahouda Gallery, Montreal, Quebec, Canada, 2007

facilitated by increasingly open "meshworks" between the physical and the virtual. There is a need for ecologies that can deal with these different realms; in other words, ecologies premised on a "second nature." As such, they would be "second-order ecologies." Conceived this way, ecology would not be the maintenance of a preexisting natural order or environment; nor is it a condition of equilibrium or balance. Rather, it would be a continual dynamic relationship between matter, energy, and information in a specific medium (environment).

Pneus

The progenitors of contemporary generative modeling and evolutionary structures include the Scottish mathematician biologist D'Arcy Wentworth Thompson and the German artist zoologist Ernst Haeckel.[7] In essence, both Thompson and Haeckel suggest that form considered contingent to environment is only a momentarily stable state or configuration (Thompson) that produces ever-changing forms; and that the multiplicity of potential cell genotypes must be a function of evolutionary or generative processes (Haeckel). In other words, the form and the nature of an organism depend on both its environment and temporal change (growth,

FIG. 04 *Diatomea*, Ernst Haeckel, Plate 84 from *Kunstformen der Natur*, 1899

evolution). Accordingly, the work of Thompson and Haeckel should be understood in terms of morphogenesis, morphology, and metabolism, rather than pure form or classification systems. [FIG. 04]

Haeckel, better known for his carefully rendered organisms and their variations in his 1904 *Artforms in Nature* and similar works, first defined the term *ecology* in 1866.[8] Clearly influenced by his contemporary, Charles Darwin, Haeckel wrote:

> By ecology we understand the study of the economy, the husbandry, of animal organisms. This means that ecology should examine all the conditions of animals, both their inorganic and organic surround-ings, above all the friendly and hostile relations with animals and plants that they directly or indirectly come into contact with; or in other words all the complex mutual relations, all the conditions that Darwin included in the expression "struggle for existence."[9]

It is perhaps not accidental that the concepts of Darwin's evolution and Haeckel's ecology were coincident; the causal interrelationships between an organism's change, growth, and transformation over time and its environment are common to both. Haeckel's concept of ecology is derived from his studies of uni- or microcellular organisms of radiolarians (ur-animals: protozoa) and diatoms (ur-plants: protophyta) in situ. They appealed to Haeckel because they were found in diverse environments under varying conditions, and were therefore emblematic of the effects of environment on the evolution of the organism. One ontological consequence of Haeckel's ecology is that the interrelations of the small and large on the one hand, and the morphogenetic and morphological on the other, can be understood as symbiotic parts of the concept from its inception, a factor that has changed little since.

The lineage of Thompson's slightly later morphological studies on the effect of environment on the growth and form of biology is traceable to Haeckel. But Thompson's work is pivotal in shifting emphasis from the formal to the morphological, as well as to the physics and mechanics of organisms. As a mathematician and biologist, Thompson approached the study of variation in organisms somewhat differently from Haeckel. His studies generally fall into what was later defined as the field of "allometry," or the scaling of animals and plants, revealing his mathematical or mechanical point of view of nature. These studies are best known to those in the design profession through Thompson's use of a geometrical coordinate system to "parametricize" and distort the shape or form of a family of fish, for example, suggesting possible environmental influences on their differing forms. At an extreme, these examples show evolutionary morphological changes that have occurred to this family or species resulting in different phyla or *embranchements* where the particular species has evolved into very distinct branches that maintain only vague morphological similarities. While these are apparently Cartesian and linear in transformation, the resulting morphological space of the transformation can be understood as a growth gradient parameter. If Thompson's simple diagrams are extrapolated, they could begin to take into account different rates of growth or changes in different parts of the fish relative to other parts. The further implication is that evolutionary change between species is produced by genetic changes in the regulatory systems governing the growth gradients as a second order parameter. [FIG. 05]

Both radiolarians and diatoms were indicative of what Haeckel referred to as "biocrystallization": organisms comprised of fundamental

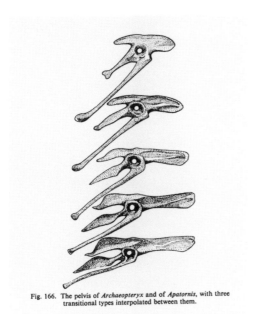

FIG. 05 Pelvis of *Archaeopteryx* and *Apatornis*, D'Arcy Wentworth Thompson, figure 166, from *On Growth and Form*, 1917

Fig. 166. The pelvis of *Archaeopteryx* and of *Apatornis*, with three transitional types interpolated between them.

platoniclike crystal forms. Thompson refers to Haeckel's biocrystallization for his explanation of the growth of organisms, and writes, in reference to the hexagonal structure of the radiolarians:

> We know that their mutual tensions will tend to conform them into the fashion of a honeycomb, or regular meshwork of hexagons.... But here a strange thing comes to light. No system of hexagons can enclose space; whether the hexagons be equal or unequal, regular or irregular, it is still under all circumstances mathematically impossible....[10]

Citing Swiss mathematician and physicist Leonhard Euler's theorem on hexagons—which, already geometrically packed on a flat plane, mathematically cannot enclose space in any volume—Thompson points to an inherent limit of Haeckel's biocrystallization concept. The American inventor Buckminster Fuller, whose geodesic domes bear a visual and structural resemblance to diatoms and radiolarians wrote, in 1965: "subvisible microscopic animal structures called radiolarians are developed by the same mathematical and structural laws as those governing the man-designed geodesic and other non-man-designed spheroidal structures in nature."[11] Intriguingly, both Haeckel's and Fuller's initial premise—universal laws that generate the inherent and apparent repetitive biocrystalline nature of the diatoms or radiolarians—worked against the actual manifestations of the radiolarians and Fuller's domes. Haeckel's radiolarians were often drawn in a mirror to enhance the symmetry of their order, thereby contradicting the principles of difference, diversity, and variation of an ecology that Haeckel had established. Additionally, Fuller's dome is not as uniform as its universality would suggest; the placement of a five-sided pentagon as a singularity in an otherwise uniform array of interconnected hexagons on the west side of his Biosphere (1967) in Montreal highlights Euler's theorem. In this context, Haeckel and, to a lesser extent, Thompson, need to be understood against their Platonic or teleological background, which sought to explain the world according to the immanence of crystalline forms. Despite their formative concepts, developed around morphogenesis and evolution, they sought to base their work in the immutable principles of mathematical and geometrical orderings, attributing specific biocrystalline properties as a fundamental building block for nature's organisms and relationships. In parallel, Haeckel's and Thompson's contemporaries theorized similar mathematical models in other fields, seeking to establish causality between the microorganism and the cosmological. This immanent and transcendent causality in science had held since before the time of German astronomer Johannes Kepler's studies of hexagonal snowflakes in the 1600s.

Thompson and Haeckel, whose ideas were contemporaneous with the Spanish architect Antonio Gaudi, have had a resurgent influence on contemporary architectural discourse, particularly on parametric and generative design strategies. Mark Burry has been instrumental in reassessing the inherent parametric design premises that underlie much of Gaudi's design for the Sagrada Familia Cathedral in Barcelona (begun 1883). Using Gaudi's inverted centenary models and the detailed resolution of structural and decorative components, Burry was able to resolve critical components into parametric forms that enabled specific computer numerical controlled (CNC) processes to speed the construction of the church.[12] This influence extends to the emergent fields of adaptive and responsive design. Biological analogues (and the biomimetic) are becoming increasingly incorporated into design strategies. This is a tendency that cannot be easily separated from either the increasing technological and digital basis of design and digital fabrication, or the increasing emphasis on ecological approaches to design that seek further integration between the built and natural environments.

The work of the Lightweight Structures Institute, established by the German architect and engineer Frei Otto in 1964, drew extensively on aspects of Haeckel's studies of radiolarians and diatoms. The institute's investigations were also heavily indebted to Thompson's *On Growth and Form*. Their fascination with the combination of pneumatic and web- or cell-like structures resulted in two seminal issues of the institute's journal, devoted exclusively to diatoms and radiolarians respectively.[13] These studies employed allometriclike operations to model and scale up the studied principles of these life-forms into possible organizational patterns, self-organizing systems (packing and density), and architectonic structures; and, investigating the interrelation between morphogenesis, a hard carapace, and softer structures, drew analogies from the organic-inorganic nature of the diatom.

The institute's work on diatoms was preceded by earlier research on pneumatic structures.[14] These studies were conducted in collaboration with biologists and derived from an interpretation of the microscopic, air- or fluid-filled cellulose structures (pneus) found in all plant matter. The studies covered such fields as generation, form metamorphosis, soft pneus, and solid pneus. Pneus—as well as providing conduits for food, nutrition, and being facilitators for photosynthesis—provide flexible and adaptable structural support and strength for the plant under times of external environmental stress, such as wind. These earlier studies, in part concluding with various pneumatic forms and inflatable structures, were more open-ended and, in many ways, not as predetermined in outcome as the studies in the later publications. Additionally, the nature of pneus, and their inherent manifoldlike characteristics given by their interconnected cellular disposition—as a conduit for energy, structure, cell system, and more—suggests that they have a distinct role to play in the design of ecologies. [FIG. 06]

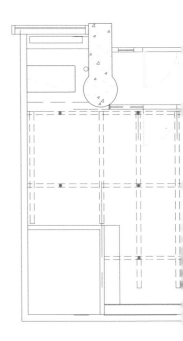

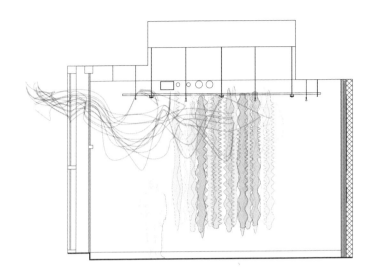

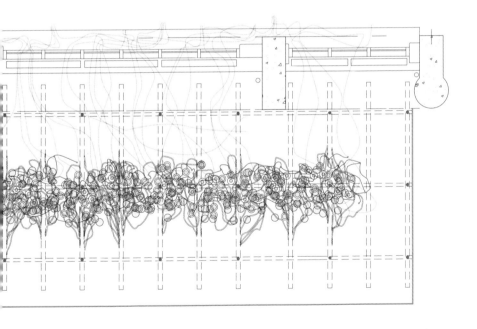

FIG. 06 Installation plan, section, and elevation, Peter Hasdell and Patrick Harrop, Pneus, Monopoli Gallery, Montreal, Quebec, Canada, 2008

Pneuma

Pneuma—neither pure practice, research, or academic pursuit—is better described as a milieu. As a loose, organizational framework, Pneuma is a project-specific collaborative vehicle I established with Patrick Harrop. This undertaking attempts, at a very concrete level, to work within an open-source framework as a means to foster a broader culture or milieu in which projects are developed and tested.[15] The development of proofs for concepts, parts, and assemblies demands an intense, collaborative, participatory hands-on process. Through prototypes, Pneuma outputs various assemblages as public installation art projects, electronic arts festivals, and in gallery installations.[16] The resultant, heterogeneous, and multiauthored outcomes have generated possibilities for a gradual exploration of an indeterminate architecture. [FIG. 07] Pneuma is developing a cellular, or soft, approach to architecture using inflatables. The history of inflatables in architecture is intrinsically connected to hot-air balloons and their predecessors, the airships and blimps of the two world wars, and owes much to the 1960s counterculture movement in which inflatable structures promised an architecture somewhat freed from the constraints of gravity, foundation, site, and permanence. Pneuma's inflatables (cells) are developed with intelligent architectures (microprocessors) to make rudimentary cellular automata, or building blocks, for a retrograde "universal constructor"—a concept developed by mathematician John Von Neumann in the 1940s for a self-replicating, logical, "machine" that could grow, evolve, and duplicate. The mutable pneumatic cells are a responsive set of physical entities with specific behaviors—physical properties, pneumatic regulation, sensory and mechanical—which are combined, then evolved and developed, for a subsequent assemblage. Successive installations place the cells in differing assemblages, directed toward manifesting larger, indeterminate, metabolic behaviors. Over time, Pneuma's work with individual cells and aggregate assemblages has developed into a complex of multiple overlaid systems: pneumatic, mechanical, sensory, and natural. The combination of these systems generates a discourse, both within the multiple pathways of interconnection and between the organic nature of the aggregate and the participant. Pneuma is not seeking predictability, but inherently emergent responses and unexpected outcomes. There is, therefore, an emphasis on

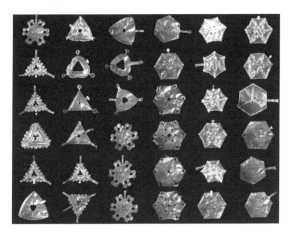

FIG. 07 Laser welded cell genotype evolution, Peter Hasdell and Patrick Harrop, Plastic Haeckel, 2007

adaptability: the open-ended possibilities and infinite variations analogous to living species inhabiting specific milieus.

Pneuma's work is situated by the two main threads explored in the text above: the morphologies of architecture (the evolution of form) and the metabolic or environmental relationships (inputs and outputs) of the assemblies. [FIG. 08] Pneuma's morphological strand draws from the generative and analogical work of Haeckel and the Lightweight Structures Institute. Pneuma's evolution of a range of inflatable cell types that are generative and mutable can therefore be positioned in relation to emerging parametric design systems and digital fabrication. Digital fabrication is currently reliant on increasingly sophisticated technologies that can have effects counter to their purported efficiencies, effective material usage, and customizing potential. For example, the ability to rapidly prototype means digital fabricators can become proliferators of excess, creating all manner of copies and prototypes in pursuit of the ideal or final component. One underinvestigated outcome, therefore, is how the proliferation of substandard or beta generations of "stuff," can be reconceptualized into a continually mutating or evolving morphology.

In one project, we configured a rapid prototyping process that replicated and mutated inflatable cells in a successive series through laser welding. In this process, each iteration of a prototype became part of a phylogeny of imperfection, a viral cell replicated and modified. When

these cells were added incrementally to a Pneuma assemblage, the resultant construct became an expanding entity that incorporated all elements, evolving and growing through continual modification to a changing set of parameters. It both contained and was shaped by the evolving and mutating components that constituted it. Component failures and genetic dead-ends were a part of it, as were "fit" elements that were able to adapt to a continually changing set of parameters and environmental conditions, including structural performance. As a result, the assemblage incorporated and encoded the processes of its formation and evolution within its matrix, creating an imperfect meshwork between the whole and its cells.[17]

Of interest in such open-ended processes are conditions and system behaviors that cannot be preconfigured or "designed" toward a functional or engineering-oriented solution. There is no plan for such an assemblage, only an algorithm. To extrapolate this in terms of possible design ecologies is to note that evolution and generative design have implications that go beyond a biomorphic approach to form making; parametric considerations are not necessarily best used as a form finding or optimizing procedure. Indeterminate generative constructs allow complex systems and structures to emerge. In the process, peculiar kinds of ecologies become inherent constituents within the body, building into the matrix an adaptive behavior whereby individual components become optimized, redundant, or points of failure—an interconnected web, or relations of cells, that could be said to either "live" or "die" as if in a game of artificial life. Such tests are small iterations, somewhat modest in scope, but they speak of a different order of thinking and doing which surely opens new possibilities.

The second key aspect of Pneuma's work derives, in part, from cybernetics and an interest in "artificial ecologies." Drawing from concepts including Maturana's and Varela's autopoiesis, Pneuma employs various overlaid systems to structure, connect, and provide input and sensory capability to the cells and the assemblage as a whole. These include: pneumatic systems, actuators, and regulators; sensory capabilities; mechanical mechanisms; and environmental variables. While rudimentary and sometimes basic (often employing simple Biology, Electronics, Aesthetics, and Mechanics robots, or BEAMbots, that mimic the behavior of natural organisms), their combination begins to effect unpredictable responses or behaviors.[18] For example, the movement of a mechanism or

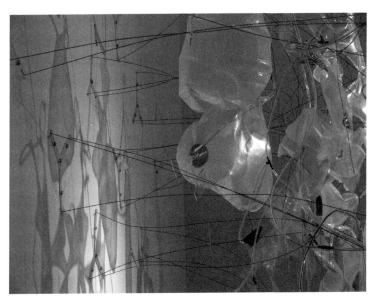

FIG. 09 Shadow projections, Peter Hasdell and Patrick Harrop, Pneuma Device, Joyce Yahouda Gallery, Montreal, Quebec, Canada, 2007

an environmental change may result in an unexpected pattern of light on a photocell, which in turn modifies some other aspect of the assemblage as a whole. This is a way to manifest larger, indeterminate metabolic behaviors within a specific assemblage or configuration. By establishing interdependencies between different levels or layers in the assemblage as a whole, a type of ecology can be designed. This operative mode is therefore rhizomatic and weedlike.

Implicitly raw, nonprescriptive, and unfinished, Pneuma has been gradually coevolving these two strands. [FIG. 09] As a vehicle, it raises questions about the design of ecologies, feedback systems, and complex, or unpredictable, behaviors. Can there, for example, be symbiosis between artificial and natural systems, using metabolic (nonlinear) systems that can work between the two? Can we develop a mode of design practice that does not become enslaved to the teleological imperatives, the technocratic paradigms, or the pathological problem solving and ethical righteousness, that characterizes much of ecological design today, but is, rather, a design approach that remains open and active? As a soft and weedy architecture, Pneuma offers one ongoing exploration of open-ended possibilities for design ecology; it is by necessity indeterminate, open sourced, incomplete, and evolving.

NOTES

1. Mathis Wakernagel and William Rees, *Our Ecological Footprint: Reducing Human Impact on the Earth* (Gabriola Island, B.C.: New Society Publishers, 1996).

2. Kevin Kelly, *Out of Control: The New Biology of Machines, Social Systems, and the Economic World* (Reading, MA: Addison-Wesley Press, 1994), 54.

3. N. Katherine Hayles, "An interview/dialogue with Albert Borgmann and N. Katherine Hayles on humans and machines" (1999), University of Chicago Press, http://www.press.uchicago.edu/Misc/Chicago/borghayl.html; Bruno Latour, *We Have Never Been Modern* (Boston: Harvard University Press, 2006).

4. International Telecommunication Union (ITU), "ITU Internet Reports 2005: The Internet of Things," November 2005, http://www.itu.int/osg/spu/publications/internetofthings.

5. Humberto Maturana and Francisco Varela, *Autopoiesis and Cognition: The Realization of the Living* (Boston: Boston Studies in the Philosophy of Science, Springer, 1980), 78.

6. Kelly, *Out of Control*, 4.

7. D'Arcy Wentworth Thompson, *On Growth and Form* (1917; revised 1942; New York: Dover, 1992).

8. Ernst Haeckel, *Kunstformen der Natur* (Leipzig and Vienna: Verlag des Bibliographischen Instituts, 1904).

9. Ernst Haeckel, *Generelle Morphologie der Organismen: allgemeine Grundzüge der organische Formen-Wissenschaft, mechanisch begründet durch die von Charles Darwin reformirte Descendenz-Theorie*, volume 1 (Berlin: G. Reimer, 1866).

10. Thompson, *On Growth and Form*, 157–60.

11. R. Buckminster Fuller, "Conceptuality of Fundamental Structures," in *Structure in Art and in Science*, ed. György Kepes (New York: George Braziller, 1965), 80.

12. Mark C. Burry, "Between Intuition and Process: Parametric Design and Rapid Prototyping," in *Architecture in the Digital Age*, ed. Branko Kolarevic (London: Spon Press, 2003), 48–162.

13. Frei Otto / Institut für leichte Flächentragwerke, *IL 33 Radiolaria: Shells in Nature and Technics II* (Stuttgart: Institut für leichte Flächentragwerke, 1990).

14. See Frei Otto / Institut für leichte Flächentragwerke, *IL 9 Pneus in nature and technics*, (1977); *IL 12 Convertible Pneus* (1975); and *IL 19 Growing and dividing Pneus* (1979). *IL 35 Pneu and bone* (1995), in part summarizes the earlier work.

15. See Peter Hasdell and Patrick Harrop, "Pneuma," www.pneumata.net; Ana Betancour and Peter Hasdell, "Architecture and Urban Design Laboratory (AR+U)," http://www.arch.kth.se/a-url; and Peter Hasdell, "Artificial Ecologies: Second Nature Emergent Phenomena in Constructed Digital—Natural Assemblages," *Leonardo Electronic Almanac* 14, no. 8 (2006), http://leoalmanac.org/journal/vol_14/lea_v14_n07-08/phasdell.asp.

16. *Pneuma Assemblage*, Artefact Urban Sculptures, Ile St Helene, Montreal (2007); *Pneuma Device*, Joyce Yahouda Gallery, Montreal (2007), *Remedios Terrarium*, FOFA Gallery, Concordia University (2008); *Pneus*, Champ Libre, Montreal (2008); and *E-sea*, Shanghai E-Arts Festival (2008).

17. Manuel De Landa, *Intensive Science & Virtual Philosophy* (London: Continuum, 2002); and Manuel De Landa, *A Thousand Years of Non Linear History* (New York: Swerve / MIT press, 1997).

18. David M. Hrynkiw and Mark W. Tilden, *Junkbots, Bugbots, and Bots on Wheels* (New York: McGraw Hill/Osborne, 2002).

Tabling Ecologies and Furnishing Performance
Stephen Turk

I use the word "table" in two superimposed senses: the nickel-plated,
rubbery table swathed in white, glittering beneath a glass sun devouring
all shadow—the table where, for an instant, perhaps forever, the umbrella
encounters the sewing-machine; and also a table, a tabula, *that enables*
thought to operate upon the entities of our world, to put them in order, to
divide them into classes, to group them according to names that designate
their similarities and their differences—the table upon which, since the
beginning of time, language has intersected space.
—Michel Foucault, The Order of Things

The Tabula: Site of the Performance of the *Oikos*

Tables are highly charged symbols in our society. We signal our willingness to negotiate by "coming to the table"; we designate status by being
placed "at the head of the table"; we show community by "gathering
around the table"; we offer ideas by "putting them on the table"; we put
those ideas aside by "tabling" them for another day; and we intoxicate ourselves by "drinking ourselves under the table." In each case, the table is a
site of action or mediation, placed in a spatial relationship to an action or
circumstance through its pairing with a preposition: to, at, over, around,
on, under. The noun pairing, "room and board"—literally a reference
to the Latin *tabula* (board) and, by extension, table—points to the centrality of the table as a focus of activity and mediator of domestic space.
So embedded is this idea in our language and thought that the spatial
surface of the table, allowing as it does for a free zone of operation among
a number of actors, serves as a metaphor of exchange. These idioms make
clear the importance of the idea of the table as a mediator of temporal and
spatial situations.

The table is thus a conceptual map of the larger spatial idea of inter-
change, and can be said to be a microcosm of the conditions of interaction in general. Tables are metaphorical reductions of larger spatial zones,

FIG. 01 Woodcut of a family dining, artist unknown, from the Roxburghe Ballads, early seventeenth century

and, as such, they share many similarities with other forms of abstraction, such as plan drawings and other orthographic projections. In this capacity, they have served as representational operators for millennia, acting as game boards, abacuses, and counting tables. Within the contemporary vocabulary of information theory, network logics, and ecology, however, the idea of tables has taken on new implications. In this context, they might be viewed as network nodes, environmental niches, contextual fields, conduits, and "places" of exchange. They are relational entities par excellence and they thus constitute, in a broad way, a model for ideas of interaction within milieus. With all of their metaphorical and spatial connotations—they open up the space of examination, determination, distribution, and dissemination among diverse participants—tables constitute a kind of network architecture.

If we narrow our focus to concentrate on domestic space, as the paradigmatic conduit of social cohesion and communication, tables can also be seen as the center of family activity. [FIG. 01] Tables have traditionally been understood as critical focal points of the home. If the hearth is the home's center of warmth and safety, the table is its center of communication and conduit of external relations. Conceived as both social and informational constructs and logistical and pragmatic systems, tables are the regulating mechanisms controlling what flows in and out of a house; the root of a distributive umbilical cord that connects the family to society at large. In short, conceived both literally and symbolically as the locus of domesticity, tables are the ecological regulators of the household. The word ecology is, of course, a compound of the roots *oikos* (household) and *logos* (knowledge). Thus the study of ecology (in this classic sense) might be best undertaken through the study of this all-important spatial and logistical regulator.

Tables, as philosopher Michel Foucault has pointed out, have had a long association with Western civilization's organization of systems of knowledge. For Foucault, the "table, a *tabula*…enables thought to operate upon the entities of our world, to put them in order, to divide them in classes, to group them according to names that designate their similarities and their differences."[1] Tables in their graphic form—as charts, diagrams, and matrices—operate as systems of organization; they are organisms, literally working engines, that through their system of rows and columns, their array of categorical distinctions, associations, and relational interconnections, produce order in the world. [FIG. 02]

That they are known as *matrices*—literally *mothers*—demonstrates the archaic and deeply paternal notion of the matron as the center of domestic life, the arranger and organizer of the household. As a metaphorical concept, a physical artifact, and a graphic construct, tables are the *embodiment* of oikos, the site of engenderment, growth, transformation, and exchange. The association between table and matrix emphasizes the multifaceted link between tables and the human figure. They persistently and curiously evoke an anthropomorphism (tables have heads and feet) that is surprising given the collective space they insinuate. Tables tend to produce an uncanny notion of a body with multiple legs (and columns and rows), a kind of monstrous multiplicity that blends bodies together.

FIG. 02 Counting tables, Gregor Reisch, *Margarita Philosophica*, 1508

Tables have always operated in a space of multiplicity—where they engender a foreign notion of a whole constituted out of other scaled wholes. They simultaneously operate as a collective, "incorporated" body—a body constituted by many other bodies (cells)—and as a unified, singular whole. This is a scaling phenomenon, generated through the property of nesting, where tables have the ability to exist inside other tables. This nesting evokes baroque constructions that operate within a schema of differentiation, through repetition and aggregation.

Because of this property of multiplicity, tables are both relational armatures and critical actors in the idea of the construction of situations. From the abacuses and counting tables of the ancients, to contemporary tables exemplified by Microsoft Excel, the table has been the performative regulator of relational data. In a sense, the recent fascination with the idea of the performative and parametric possibilities of architecture has been prefigured, for millennia, by the latent transactional possibilities of the table: first, as an actual physical object, providing for a space of action, and, then, as a conceptual graphic construct. Tables are such critical performative structures in our society it is not so difficult to suggest they might serve as a basis for the investigation of a relational understanding of *design ecologies*, not only in the domestic sense discussed above, but also, in an era of globalization and networked information, as a locus for relational strategies of connectivity and flow regulation in general.

As an ecological regulator, the table is a kind of performer. Tracing the interconnection between the idea of performance and furnishing is an avenue for understanding the idea of tables as ecological operators. The etymology of the word *performance* helps elucidate this concept: the word comes down to us from the Latin *per-* + *fournir* (to furnish)—to furnish or deliver in full—via the postclassical Latin *perfurnire*, the Old French *parfornir*, the Anglo-Norman *performer*, and the Middle English *performen*.[2] Performance thus means something akin to "of the furniture or furnishing." At its root, then, performance simply means to furnish or provide, and, by implication, the performer is that person who does the supplying. Additionally, there is an implied sense of temporality and spatiality; the supplying of a need or desire occurs at particular locations and specific times, and the satisfaction of desire is almost always dependent on these spatiotemporal factors. This spatiotemporal implication is what allowed the word to drift toward its present connotation: an object providing comfort within a room.

Furnishing Responses: The Typology of the *Oikos*

Tables have a role in regulating what the household consumes, whether that is measured at the traditional scale of the individual nuclear family, the neighborhood, the town, the city, or the world. For the ancient Greeks, oikos came to refer not just to the literal household, but to the city-state itself. [FIG. 03] The city, with all its functional characteristics, was seen as a kind of political, social, and economic family. As the site of a vectorial exchange of the forces of provision, tables act as a neutral vessel, relational system, or node. As an idea that can be abstracted to any number of scales, tables have come, as representational armatures, to metaphorically stand in for these multiple scales. This scaling of the metaphorical implications of oikos can be extended in both the macro and micro directions, further abstracting the idea into a kind of parametric operator.

The recent focus of architectural design has, as is well known, moved from a fascination with critical theory and language to notions of practice and performance. The focus has shifted toward the consideration of architectural objects within larger fields of operation—the milieu or ecology in which a design exists. Indeed, it is not so clear that we are dealing with the simple design of objects; the boundary between an object and its environment has been progressively eroded over the last century, a fact which is

FIG. 03 Typical Greek houses, fifth through third century BCE, drawn by Stephen Turk after drawings in Bertha Carr Rider, *Ancient Greek Houses: Their History and Development from the Neolithic Period to the Hellenistic Age* (Cambridge: Cambridge University Press, 1916)

reminiscent of how the idea of the oikos was extended by the ancients. Contemporary designers consider the ecological context in which an organism (the design itself) is formed; they consider how it evolves out of the forces embedded in a contextual field. Designers have thus become more interested in the possibility of producing what amounts to customized organisms. The very strategy of design presumes a system for continued evolution and responsive intelligence in any developed solution. Design is now understood as a process of unfolding possibilities within an ecological or contextual system; it is a kind of performance in which the designed organisms *furnish responses* to the dynamic field conditions of the environment.

To a significant degree, architect Greg Lynn can be credited for the renewed interest in the contextual forces acting on design, conceived as a kind of responsive system. The return to the archaic notions of the animate and "virtual" (a reference to the archaic sense of power and force) in Lynn's early essays, and his interest in cybernetic theory—the study of the structure of organisms' regulatory feedback systems—refocused attention on the primary importance of the body and materiality in architectural process and thought.[3] However, the body that architects are now interested in is one fully embedded in its milieu where its material performance—and thus its performative nature—is a result of the ebb and flow of forces. It is also a body, which is no longer an ideal classical whole, but a posthumanist assembly of aggregated systems: organisms inside other organisms, echoing the baroque interest in nested realities and the scalability of the oikos metaphor. Lynn is fond of evoking American biologist Lynn Margulis's notions of bodies as collections of organisms, a position which places his ideas firmly in the realm of posthumanist thinking. According to Lynn, for Margulis, "there is little difference between a single body and an ecology of organisms, as both exploit one another's functions and machinic behaviors through feedback and exchange."[4]

This renewed interest in the body as a kind of ecology is related to Foucault's idea of the power of the table to order and divide the entities of the world into classes, to name them, and designate their similarities and differences. It is against this naming and organizing property that thinkers such as Margulis position themselves. So too, the computational and biological infatuations of contemporary architectural practice have extended these interests. In its shift to the performative, architecture has moved its attention from the transcendental and heroic projects of modernism to a more situational and material understanding of architecture as a performative act, a kind of choreography of active systems in the environment. Indeed choreography (the articulation of the performative) may be an apt metaphorical condition for a number of shifts in architectural theory over the past several decades.

The question of type has been radically reevaluated in this new understanding. Formally a central question in the establishment of the notion of ideal formal relationships and patterns, the concept has recently undergone a shift, which places emphasis on mutability and transience and resists notions of stasis and fixed identity. Type exists, but only as a contingent and mutable reality subject to the changes of contexts and fields. The fixed state of any organism—and, by extension, design object—is not a permanent condition, but a momentary example of homeostasis and equilibrium, the result of certain contextual balances in forces affecting any organism. What might seem to be a fixed characteristic of a group of organisms is, if viewed from a larger, temporal perspective, a moment in the trajectory of a transforming set of morphological changes or evolving characteristics. This is, of course, an idea central to cybernetic theories of the development of organisms. We are seeing the full impact of these ideas on architectural theory only now, nearly a half-century after their appearance in other disciplines.

As we have seen above, the idea of performance has always had a latent architectural and spatial underpinning. Its full-fledged reemergence into the center of architectural thought reactivates a set of ancient metaphors; a renewed investigation of the historical implications of performance is critical to understanding its appearance within the discipline of architecture. The question, following these developments, becomes: What is being supplied in this architectural performance? The supply of objects, divisions, order, rhythm, repetition, difference, energy, mood, sustenance, or even meaning itself are perhaps all possibilities. The supplying of things (objects) might literally imply the staging of the landscape on which a performance appears—the stagecraft associated with a space of performance. This is a connection, which seems to link it directly with the root *fournir*, the literal furnishing of a space, where the production of furniture, formally considered a minor mode of architectural practice, becomes a major concern.

The Wave Table Project: Performance, Usefulness, and the Limitations of the Ecology of Type

Once noticed, it continued to occupy one's mind. It even persisted, as it were, in going about its own business.... The striking thing was that it was neither simple nor really complex, initially or intentionally complex, or constructed according to a complicated plan. Instead, it had been desimplified in the course of its carpentering.... As it stood, it was a table of additions, much like certain schizo-phrenics' drawings, described as "overstuffed," and if finished it was only in so far as there was no way of adding anything more to it, the table having become more and more an accumulation, less and less a table.... It was not intended for any specific purpose, for anything one expects of a table. Heavy, cumbersome, it was virtually immovable. One didn't know how to handle it (mentally or physically). Its top surface, the useful part of the table, having been gradually reduced, was disappearing, with so little relation to the clumsy framework that the thing did not strike one as a table, but as some freak piece of furniture, an unfamiliar instrument...for which there was no purpose....A table that lent itself to no function....
—Henri Michaux, The Major Ordeals of the Mind

The literal examination of the typological class "table" is a fitting place to begin an exploration of the arguments raised above—to address the relationship between performance and furnishing in a pragmatic and direct way—especially because tables have such historically strong ties to notions of typology. The category "table" seems stable and self-evident. Discussions of table design typically center on questions of typology and its relationship to conventional notions of use: tables are defined relative to their relationship to program and function and the corresponding collection of design elements, which contribute to their classifications. The table, then, especially when seen in light of the discussion above, is ripe for an examination of the limits of its typological variation.

The strategy of such an investigation points to the need to understand the philosophical implications of the metaphorical association of tables with concepts of knowledge and the body. A design project, centered on the relationship between tables and an expanded sense of ecology, needs to take into account the question of how types are defined by the contextual niches into which these design organisms fall.

With these questions in mind, I began the Wave Table Project in 2005 as an exploration of the defining boundaries of the table type and a study in the range of table forms. [FIG. 04] By producing what amounts to a "near-table"—an object that does not fall exactly into the stereotypical definition of table, but at the same time possesses all the classical characteristics of a table—the project makes a broader critique of classification systems, based on the typological classification of performative characteristics. The project resists simple typological configurations and seriously explores the possibility of responsive iterative systems that look at the "ecologies" of specific uses of table "classes." The individual production

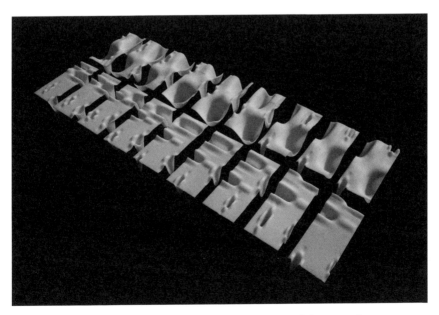

FIG. 04 Table sequences from series i and j, Stephen Turk, Wave Table Project, 2008

FIG. 05 Wave Table prototypes, series j variations, Stephen Turk, Wave Table Project, 2008

of table examples is understood as part of a larger mutable set of tables that explore both the limits of the classical table definition as well as the bounds of programmatic distinctions that might be termed usefulness and uselessness. The program of table is no longer fixed in this study; like an organism in a milieu, it takes on different performative possibilities in different contexts, whereby each example is designed as a symbolic registration of a field of forces.

In many ways, then, the Wave Table Project contemplates the relationship between use and taxonomy and plays upon the boundary between actual tables and metaphorical abstractions. We conceive and name components of an object by reference to function and, often, by metaphorical association with body elements or actions. The set of tables produced in this project is intended to question the notion of what is "useful" in a table through the blurring of the distinction between these formal and functional types. As formal and functional types begin to break down there is a corresponding breakdown in our ability to name them. For example, as the legs of the Wave Tables take on attributes of the table-top—the useful surface and location of a table's program—we are less able to name this morphological feature as it is neither simply a tabletop nor a leg. [FIG. 05] It is by this method that the project explores the role of the table as an "ecological" regulator within domestic situations.

The project is interested in a critique of typological and cladistic systems in general and intends to suggest a potential or latent ambiguity within these systems. *Cladistics* is a term borrowed from evolutionary theory and used to describe branching classification systems which constantly subdivide to define new distinctions in a system of differences; an

organizing system best exemplified by a tree diagram of speciation
(a phylogenetic or "Tree of Life" diagram). The project proposes to substi-
tute these discrete divisions with vague operators such as those provided
in language by suffix constructions, such as *-ish*, *-ness*, and *-esque*, which,
for example, result in such terms as *tableish* or *tablesque*, the condition
of being near, like, or similar to a typological condition known as table.
By questioning the possibility of deriving distinctions by division into discrete branches, the project argues for a continuity of blurred change.

This blurring of formally distinct component types unifies the performance of use with the structure of the table itself. In these examples, the
table has no separate legs or other secondary components. Each table is
a surface through which an external force is applied to produce a kind of
"surface solid," unifying what was formally conceived as differentiated
elements of skin and bone. The Wave Tables are conceived as a family,
a kind of oikos, produced in a series that allows for parametric variation:
a lineage of smoothly changing differentiation in individuals. As the surface and the structural components are undifferentiated, elements such
as legs can be modified and produced as needed by particular contextual
relationships. For example, the table could "grow" more legs in circumstances that call for more strength in particular locations, or fewer legs
could be used where accessibility was critical.

The project's formal logic functions through the use of what might be
termed the gizmo effect. [FIG. 06] The system operates vis-à-vis a software
displacement procedure, using what is often termed a gizmo in digital
animation systems. Gizmos are "second order abstractions" that operate
within the mathematical world of an animation system as a container of
information that is separate from, but acts upon, the visible objects in a
scene. They transfer and store data about the manipulation and transformation of an object described in space and time. In this sense they
have similarities with the notions of table discussed above. Just as the
table can be understood as an abstract placeholder for exchange, gizmos
are abstract entities that provide a "space" (really a database entry point
or "cell" in a program table) for the registration and storage of data in
animation software. They are usually represented in these systems as a
wireframe cube or rectilinear "bounding box" that is hidden from view
until needed.

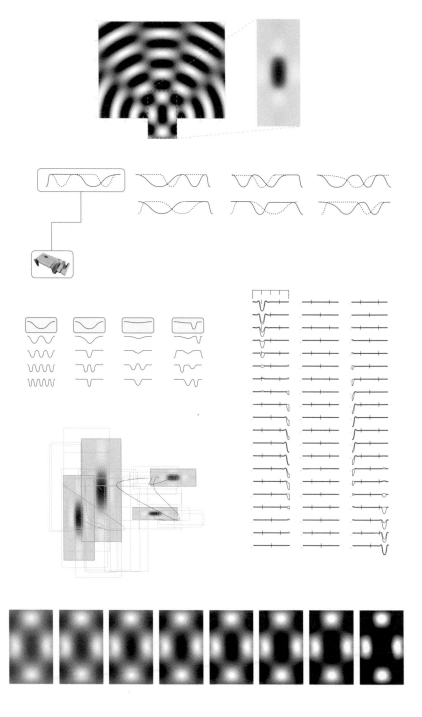

FIG. 06 Wave Table systems diagrams, Stephen Turk, Wave Table Project, 2008

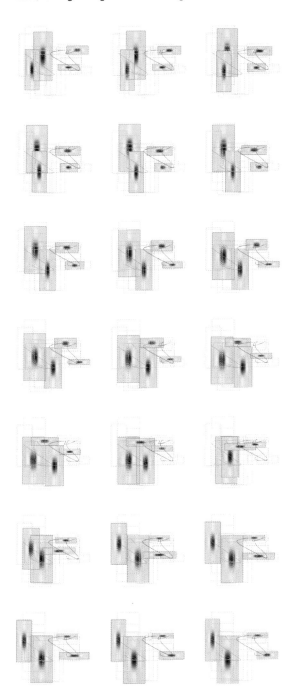

FIG. 07 Wave Table deformation path choreography diagrams, j series, Stephen Turk, Wave Table Project, 2008

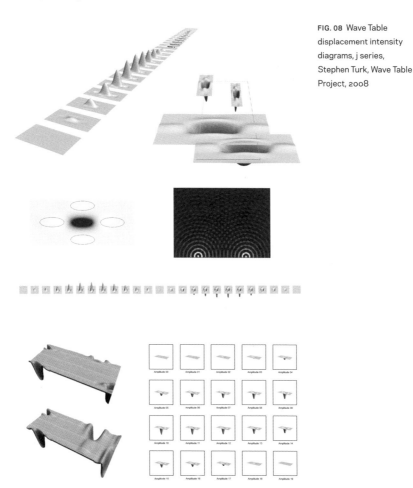

The performance of program in the Wave Table Project is a result of the scalar variation of the gizmo in the wave form modification system. The program performs relative to the displacement systems strength and the zone of effect of the gizmo. [FIG. 07] Controlling and articulating the zone of effect of the gizmo and its resulting transformations on the morphology allows for variations in the table family to emerge. The displacement itself is governed by an image displacement mechanism. In this particular case, the image is sampled from an interference pattern, derived from the classic experiment, which made evident the wave/particle duality of electromagnetic radiation. The displacements produced by this image are then "tuned" by modifying their length, width, period, and amplitude to produce distortions that take on various programmatic and structural roles in the performance of the table. [FIG. 08] Their displacement is itself a kind of performance, which is modified and animated in the software.

Individual "cells" of the animation sequence can then be sampled and topographically sectioned to produce the necessary template sections to physically fabricate any particular table instance from this sequence of animation. The sequence of cells thus acts like the evolutionary trajectory of a table family, and the table production method operates as an ecology of viable examples, as tables can be sampled out of the evolving sequence and tested for their performative characteristics. Indeed their viability and aesthetic effects can be directly tested and the results fed back into the animation system to produce new sequences of tables producing additional evolutionary lines, much like cell strains are colonized and kept for their various characteristics and genetic traits.

The Wave Table Project is not intended to answer any specific aspect of the issues raised here, but rather, like any design project, its purpose is to explore issues and evoke possibilities. In the spirit of basic scientific research, this project seeks to explore fundamental relationships and open up new avenues of exploration and awareness. In pursuing the logic of "tabling ecologies," I hope to offer an escape from conventional notions of the nature of furnishing and thereby broaden the perspective of what constitutes an "ecological" condition.

NOTES

Epigraph 1 Michel Foucault, *The Order of Things: An Archaeology of the Human Sciences* (New York: Vintage Books, 1970), xvii.

Epigraph 2 Henri Michaux, *The Major Ordeals of the Mind, and the Countless Minor Ones*, trans. Richard Howard (New York: Harcourt Brace Jovanovich, 1974), 125–26.

1. Michel Foucault, *The Order of Things: An Archaeology of the Human Sciences* (New York: Vintage Books, 1970), xvii.

2. *American Heritage Dictionary* (Boston, MA: Houghton Mifflin, 2006).

3. Greg Lynn, *Folds, Bodies & Blobs: Collected Essays* (Brussels: La Lettre Volée, 1998).

4. Greg Lynn, *Animate Form* (New York: Princeton Architectural Press, 1999), 33.

Public Farm 1 (P.F.1)

Amale Andraos
and Dan Wood
of WORKac

Since 2000, the Museum of Modern Art in New York (MoMA) and its sister institution, the P.S.1 Contemporary Art Center, have hosted the annual Young Architects Program, a competition to design a temporary installation in the courtyard of P.S.1 as a backdrop for their summer Warm Up parties. These events bring together, year after year, the best of summer fun with the latest in art, music, and architectural experimentation.

While celebrating invention, previous structures have all answered the competition's programmatic requirement to provide shade, seating, and water, while at the same time organizing P.S.1's courtyard spaces to create various zones of gathering and experience. Every intervention during the previous eight years of the competition has expanded upon the Warm Up's essential DNA: the celebrated "urban beach."

Intrigued by the infinitely open competition brief, we set ourselves to question this underlying theme of the "urban beach." Throughout the twentieth century, the beach embodied popular dreams of pleasure and liberation. From the first paid holidays for laborers—when throngs of bathers in blue-and-white-striped bathing suits invaded still-undomesticated beaches, captured in a famous photo of Coney Island from 1928—to the slogan of May 1968, "*Sous les Pavés la Plage*" (Beneath the pavement, the beach), the beach has been synonymous with the possibility of reclaiming a lost paradise.

Reflecting on our cities today, we embraced the summer of 2008, exactly forty years after '68 and eighty years after '28, as a perfect time to channel past revolutionary zeal and explore possible new symbols of liberation, knowledge, and power, combined with the lightness and play that the P.S.1 competition invited. Leaving behind the "urban beach," our project became the "urban farm"—a magical plot of rural delights which, inserted within the city grid, resonated as an appropriate expression of our generation's preoccupations with and hopes for a different and better future. With cities finally proven superior to their suburban counterparts—in everything from quality of life to environmental impact—our project became an invitation to engage urbanity, to once again make our cities much-needed laboratories of experimentation: opening minds and senses toward better living, with each other and the world. [FIG. 01]

While the history of the urban farm is long and varied, its potential to perfectly embody the intersection of ecology and urbanism—fueled by recent developments in organic and biodynamic farming, engineered soils, and other new and rediscovered technologies—today renders the urban farm a perfect starting point for a new kind of sustainable city.

Set in contrast to industrial farming—which pollutes large swathes of the rural landscape while creating mass-produced vegetables that taste only of the supermarket aisle—we proposed P.F.1 (Public Farm 1), a self-sustaining, self-regulating, and multidimensional productive garden. Rather than petroleum fertilizers and the 3,000 miles (4,800 kilometers) the average American meal travels from farm to plate, P.F.1 provided tasty, organically grown, summer-fresh fruit and vegetables within walking distance of the P.S.1 cafe. In our postindustrial age of information, customization, and individual expression, we believe the most exciting and promising developments are no longer those of mass production, but rather those of local intervention.

Channeling the last utopian architectural projects about the city— those that examined its potential, represented its promises of liberation, and captured its pleasures—P.F.1 is an architectural and urban manifesto, to engage play and reinvent our cities once again. It is an experiment in what we call "rurbalization," a revamped Jeffersonian ideal, where the urban fuses with the rural, density is combined with open space, food production meets consumption, and even town life and cosmopolitanism coexist. It opens cities and urban denizens to new pleasures—from farmers' markets, to vegetal roofs, to chickens in the parks. Celebrating the ability of cities to mix, layer, and compress, P.F.1 is an attempt to further densify the city, bringing the systems and infrastructure that sustain cities from their periphery to their heart, appropriating and transforming them to create new and unexpected spaces for program and social interaction. [FIG. 02]

Section

For P.F.1 to truly express its urban condition, it was imperative the project engage its section. Attempting to coalesce both the diversity of city life and the duality of the program—a working farm combined with a party space for up to seven thousand people—we sought a design that would allow the farm to coexist sectionally with activities, spaces, and experiences beneath.

One of the dreams of the '60s, since abandoned, was the concept of the megastructure—a structure so large that traditional distinctions between architecture, urbanism, and infrastructure become blurred. The structures commonly took the form of enormous, miles-long cities that spanned huge bodies of water, stretched from mountaintop to mountaintop, or hovered over existing cities, always projecting an optimistic vision of society's future in contrast with the cities of old. We adopted a minimegastructure as the overall formal organization of the project, inserting within the P.S.1 courtyards a single floating shape, a kind of "farm-bridge," positioned in such a way that it created different spaces and zones of occupation. This form not only resonated with visionary urban projects of the past—from Superstudio's Continuous Monument (1969) to Yona Friedman's Ville Spatiale (1958)—it also embodied our desire to rethink infrastructure and ecological *systems* as potentially integral to architectural expression.

This nod to the streamlined vision of the megastructure was then subjected to a number of twists. The first replaced the cool architectural grid explored in the autonomous projects of generations past with the very real and living agricultural grid, a time-honored way to organize crops. The second was born in the realization that our original idea of the "farm-bridge" would have distinct disadvantages: the crops could not be seen from the ground, and the weight of the structure, plants, soil, and water would be enormous. We therefore *folded* the bridge so that the middle of the structure touched and was supported directly by the ground. This single gesture allowed views up to the farm while creating a multitude of spaces below, from kid-sized and more intimate zones near the middle of the structure, to more monumental moments at its ends, where the structure rose toward the sky. [FIG. 03]

At the center of the farm, where the structure touched the ground, we placed a pool, from which visitors could obtain views up along the crops

FIGS. 01-02 P.S.1's Summer Warm Up party, WORKac, Public Farm 1 (P.F.1), P.S.1 Contemporary Art Center, Queens, New York, 2008 Photos by Raymond Adams

from within. We aligned the axis of the pool and the fold in the structure with Long Island City's only skyscraper, a green-tinted glass tower, so that the marriage of farm and city was made all that much more explicit. [FIG. 04]

Structure

As it was a temporary installation, we wanted to build with sustainable materials. The list of inexpensive structural elements that are also biodegradable and made from recycled materials is extremely short. The unassuming cardboard tube used on construction sites for pouring concrete met those criteria. We worked closely with our structural engineers—Dan Sesil, Matt Melrose, and Pat Hopple of LERA—to create a structural grid based on the diameters of standard cardboard tubes. Sesil took our early grid sketches and created a cellular pattern of circles that fit seamlessly together in a repeatable grid. The basic module consisted of a central tube thirty inches in diameter, flanked by two twenty-eight-inch diameter tubes and two thirty-four-inch diameter tubes in a roughly hexagonal shape. This unit was termed the "daisy."

FIG. 03 The Fundernearth, WORKac, Public Farm 1 (P.F.1), P.S.1 Contemporary Art Center, Queens, New York, 2008

FIG. 04 The pool, WORKac, Public Farm 1 (P.F.1), P.S.1 Contemporary Art Center, Queens, New York, 2008

FIG. 05 Daisy "picking holes," WORKac, Public Farm 1 (P.F.1), P.S.1 Contemporary Art Center, Queens, New York, 2008   FIG. 06 The Kids' Grotto, WORKac, Public Farm 1 (P.F.1), P.S.1 Contemporary Art Center, Queens, New York, 2008

The central tube of each daisy was either left as an open tube or extended to meet the ground as a column. The daisy pattern also became our planting grid, each daisy containing a single crop. The empty tubes became "picking holes" through which urban farmers could ascend to tend to the plants. [FIG. 05]

Program

Moving under and around P.F.1, visitors could interact with a number of "column experiences" that were designed according to the position of each column within the courtyards, as well as the height and perceived scale of the cardboard structure at each point.

The Farmers' Market, located under the short wing of the farm, was organized around a solar-powered juicer, on a bright-yellow shelf, that provided fresh veggie cocktails during events, and a column wrapped in parachute fabric and entirely covered with protruding pockets that held dried herbs and other yields from the weekly harvest.

Closer to the center of the structure, where it folded down to touch the ground, the Kids' Grotto featured a fire-truck-red periscope that provided close-up views of the daisy fields from the ground. [FIG. 06] Adjacent to the pool, a towel column allowed kids to dry off, and a water-spouting fountain filtered and recirculated the pool water. At the pool perimeter, a series of lower tubes were created for "wet seating."

In the gathering of treelike columns at the P.S.1 entrance we called the Grove, smaller-diameter, cantilevered tubes were slid into the structural columns for seating and to create a series of cardboard "branches" used to grow herbs. Spinning fans, hung from above, set on a random timer, intermittently wafted the scent of herbs down to the crowds below. Two columns joined with a bench and wrapped in a bright-yellow curtain provided a place of private escape from the dancing and the music. The bench proved to be one of the most popular spots during the parties.

In the smaller courtyard, at the moment where the farm reached its most monumental point, a series of experiential columns were designed to create the Funderneath—our way of bringing animals to the farm. [FIG. 07] Barnyard sounds recorded at the Queens County Farm Museum randomly emitted from one column, while another contained peepholes

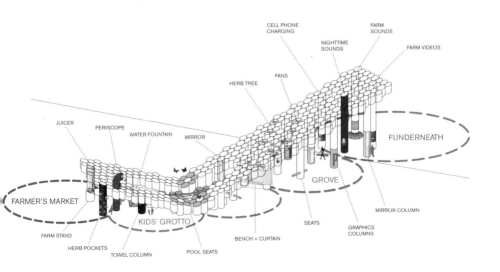

FIG. 07 Program diagram, WORKac, Public Farm 1 (P.F.1), P.S.1 Contemporary Art Center, Queens, New York, 2008

with close-up video of sheep, pigs, ducks, and goats. A painted, dark-blue "nighttime" column held chirping cricket sounds and a constellation of light-emitting diodes (LEDs) above, allowing one to see the stars at any time of the day. Finally, a solar-powered phone-charging station allowed visitors and partygoers to recharge their phones as the evening dragged on. Often, a phone would be left to recharge, only to be found filled with snapshots of the party taken by someone else.

Planting

P.F.1's herbs, fruit, and vegetables were selected to thrive in the very hot conditions created by P.S.1's courtyard in the summer. The result was a diverse mix of twenty-three types and fifty-one varieties planted to bloom in succession throughout the season. As it was important for urban farmers to have their hands free, we designed a special "Picking Skirt" for ease of movement while in midair. The skirt could be attached to hooks around the rim of each tube when working and filled, like a kangaroo's pouch, with weeds or harvested vegetables. When finished, the urban farmer

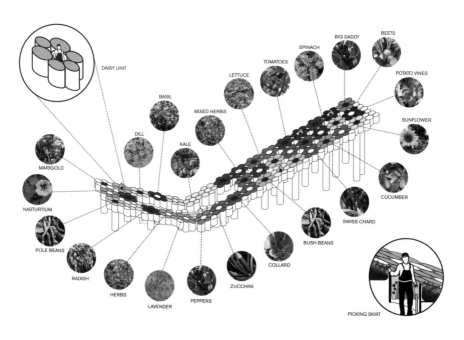

FIG. 08 Planting diagram, WORKac, Public Farm 1 (P.F.1), P.S.1 Contemporary Art Center, Queens, New York, 2008

used clips attached to the skirt to fold the skirt back on itself creating an all-surrounding "pocket" filled with produce or weeds, before descending back to the ground. [FIG. 08]

Most of the seeds for the farm were initially planted in the greenhouse of the Queens County Farm Museum, under the guidance of Michael Grady Robertson, the farm's agricultural supervisor. As they outgrew the trays they were first planted in, and then the larger pots they were transplanted to, the plants were moved to P.S.1's courtyard and into fabric containers called Smart Pots, custom designed to fit the three different tube diameters. The Smart Pots contained a growing medium, a layer of jute, and two inches of compost. Two days before the opening, the Smart Pots were lifted into the structure, following the planting daisy pattern. On the underside of the structure, each tube was given a spray-painted label so that varieties could be identified from below.

Throughout the summer, the farm was maintained with the help of the Horticultural Society of New York's GreenTeam, made up of graduates of the society's GreenHouse program, a rehabilitative program that offers intensive, six-month horticultural courses at the Rikers Island jail facility. [FIG. 09] Along with the planting at Queens County Farm Museum, 25 percent of P.F.1's plants were pregrown at Rikers' greenhouse.

The farm produce was used in the P.S.1 cafe, as well as distributed to the staff of P.S.1, WORKac, and volunteers throughout the summer, significantly reducing the distance our food had to travel.

Details

In addition to the P.S.1 courtyards and the greenhouses on Rikers Island and at Queens Farm, construction was carried out in a fourth location. Because the cardboard tubes needed to be lacquered before being exposed to the weather, we could not afford to work outside during the wet spring. A rented 10,000-square-foot (930-square-meter) warehouse in Greenpoint, Brooklyn, became our "tube-cutting factory." Up to forty volunteers painted, cut, and assembled the tubes into daisy modules under the supervision of Art Domantay, an artist and art-installer who masterminded a series of ingenious jigs and assembly-line techniques.

Tweaking common structural engineering software, LERA invented a way to model the reactions of the all-paper structure. The shelves

FIG. 09 Farm maintenance, WORKac, Public Farm 1 (P.F.1), P.S.1 Contemporary Art Center, Queens, New York, 2008

designed to support the plants became one of the key elements of the structural integrity of the tubes, providing lateral stability in their weak axis. We combined planting shelves with donut-shaped, nonplanting shelves, designed to maintain the transparency of the nonplanter tubes while providing the necessary structural stability. All the shelves were CNC-milled. A central hole was incorporated to provide drainage.

All connections were bolted. Each bolt passed through a two-by-four that was glued and screwed to the interior of the tube to provide a stiff surface to tighten the bolt against. With most tubes connecting to six others, we rapidly determined that, with the extreme weight of the soil, plants, and water, we would need tens of thousands of bolts (eight per connection) for the structure to support the more than 80,000-pound (36,000-kilogram) load.

Facing a financial and scheduling disaster, we were approached at almost exactly the right moment by Paul Mankiewicz, the inventor of a product called GaiaSoil. GaiaSoil is made from recycled industrial styrofoam, coated in a highly absorbent, natural pectin gel, that is mixed with high-grade compost to create an ultralightweight growing medium.

Invented for urban farming but never tested, Mankiewicz offered it to the project. GaiaSoil reduced the overall design load by 70 percent and the number of bolts per connection to three, *saving* the project.

Water and Power

A drip irrigation system was designed to deliver a controlled amount of water to each planter tube. A series of drip tubes with adjustable emitters branched off four main irrigation lines (2,000 feet [600 meters] of tube in all). The system was fed by a rainwater cistern, donated and installed by the Mayor's Council on the Environment NYC, which collected more than 6,000 gallons (22,000 liters) of water from the roofs of P.S.1 over the summer. A solar-powered pump moved the rainwater up through a column and throughout the farm. Another pump, hidden in one of the pool's seats, recirculated the water from the pool to the fountain-spout. All of P.F.1's equipment was solar powered. The solar power system consisted of an array of eighteen photovoltaic modules, sixteen of which were dedicated to a twenty-four-volt DC system and two of which were dedicated to a twelve-volt DC system. The twenty-four-volt system went through a charge controller, then to an inverter, transforming it into 120-volt AC that was utilized by all of P.F.1's AC appliances: fans, juicer, mister, and irrigation pumps. The twelve-volt DC system went through another charge controller and was used by all of P.F.1's DC power loads: videos screens, speakers, lights, and cell-phone chargers. Ten lead-acid batteries provided storage for these two systems, creating a truly off-the-grid installation. On overcast days, or at night, loads drew their power from the batteries. On sunny days, loads derived their power directly from the solar panels. In a nod to earlier visionaries, we designed the "shed" containing the batteries and inverters in a very humble homage to Russian constructivist Vladimir Tatlin's Monument to the Third International (1919), utilizing leftover cardboard tubes.

Chickens

The smallest of P.S.1's courtyards, room-size, became the locus for our infrastructure. We roofed it with the solar panels and channeled the piping from surrounding roofs and drains to the 800-gallon (3,000-liter) cistern, which we placed at the room's center. We stored tools there and

FIG. 10 Chickens party in the courtyard, WORKac, Public Farm 1 (P.F.1), P.S.1 Contemporary Art Center, Queens, New York, 2008

built a lockable door. Surreptitiously we were also creating a chicken coop, complete with cardboard-tube roosts. On opening night we introduced six mature chickens and twenty irresistible chicks to the farm, without informing MoMA or P.S.1. [FIG. 10] Immediately embraced by the museum, staff, and visitors, our chickens had the run of the courtyards during week-days and produced hundreds of eggs over the course of the summer.

Collaboration

P.F.1 was designed and built over a four-month period with contributions by more than 150 people and organizations who donated time, materials, or financial assistance to the project. At times, more than sixty volunteer architects from around the country and the world were working on site. Through the project we were introduced to environmentalists, farmers, horticulturists, worm-composting "kings," gardening societies, scientists studying paper, artists, golf course irrigators, and Alaskan-trained, "off-the-grid" solar specialists. Our project, initially only concerned with *ideas*, rapidly became a project about true and exhilarating *collaboration*, often with people and expertise far removed from traditional architecture and urban planning. [FIG. 11]

Post Life

At the end of the summer, P.F.1 was dismantled and its various parts donated through a "garage sale" to schools, community gardens, and other public and private institutions within New York.

Portions of this essay were previously published on http://www.work.ac.

FIG. 11 WORKac, Public Farm 1 (P.F.1), P.S.1 Contemporary Art Center, Queens, New York, 2008

Float On:
A Succession
of Progressive
Architectural
Ecologies
Scott Colman

Leading twentieth-century architects frequently and enthusiastically engaged biology in connection with the important issues of
architectural and urban structure, form, and morphology. Yet it is in
progressive architecture's embrace of the multidisciplinary, vicissitu-
dinous field of planning that the discipline's engagement with evolving
conceptions of ecology has arguably been most extensive and most
fraught. Moreover, insofar as planning has been at or near the center of
progressive architecture's historic engagement with ecological thought,
what might be called progressive architectural ecology has been dialecti-
cally intertwined with broad, contemporaneous sociopolitical movements
and their fate. Progressive architectural thought and production has both
contributed and responded to prevailing conceptions of agency, and this
has greatly affected the discipline's very conception of the environment
and its own environmental potency. Indeed, the relative political inef-
ficacy of progressive thought in the last decades of the twentieth century
has meant ecological design has increasingly become a de facto mode of
planning today.

The general, late-modern crisis of progressive agency was felt particularly strongly in the reactionary positions against modernist architecture
and urbanism in the 1960s and 1970s. Yet in much subsequent architectural production, particularly the Dutch work of the 1990s and early 2000s,
the question of agency has become a central concern for those in the discipline attempting to work architecture out of the conservative turn that
profited from the crisis of modernism. Often implicit, though of crucial
importance in this recent work, has been the need to develop strategies
that reconstitute the modernist embrace of planning in the context of
neoliberalism on the one hand, and the increasingly broad engagement
with environmental activism on the other. Equally important has been the
need to address the underlying failure of twentieth-century progressivism,
in which rational, empiricist thought failed to adequately account for the

agency of sensibility and the disequilibrating effects of ineluctable socio-cultural and environmental change.

At its best, contemporary progressive practice claims neither professional planning's position of objective representation nor its determining efficacy, but instead participates in evoking and enacting potential social and environmental performance. This shift from detached assertion to circumscribed engagement is consistent with a broader epistemic transformation: rather than an instrument of politics, economics, and sociology, the environment is becoming the empirical medium through which political, economic, and social movements are thought and, increasingly, designed. By focusing the discussion around architectural projects that, as bookends to postmodernism, have sought a direct engagement with ecology, this essay seeks to sketch out the broad characteristics of this historical transformation. The asserted value of the concept of progressive architectural ecology is that it conceives a horizon for diverse contemporary work that, manifest at all scales of practice and collected under various subdisciplines, might nevertheless be evaluated for the broadly singular character of agency in its response to the socio-environmental challenges of our time.

Modern Analogical Ecologies

In 1972, the Hungarian-American artist and theorist György Kepes published a project by his student, the young Spanish architect Juan Navarro Baldeweg, one of a number of historical and contemporary works Kepes used to illustrate his essay "The Artist's Role in Environmental Self-Regulation." Navarro Baldeweg's "Proposals for the increasing of ecological experiences" was comprised of photomontages representing large, transparent, domelike bubbles within various extant landscapes. Kepes published two Navarro Baldeweg images. One showed three bubbles in New York harbor floating against the backdrop of the Manhattan skyline. [FIG. 01] In the other, a single bubble floats among rock and ice in an arctic fjord. [FIG. 02] Although the contents of the bubbles appear indeterminate—a cloudlike substance—the image caption asserts the bubbles contain ecosystems; the project constitutes a globally circulating, waterborne gallery of ecologies designed to affect environmental awareness:

FIG. 01 Ecosystems floating in New York Harbor, Juan Navarro Baldeweg, project, 1972

FIG. 02 A tropical forest in an arctic landscape, Juan Navarro Baldeweg, project, 1972

The photomontages show possibilities of extending the concept of
a park and a botanical garden. Tundra, grassland, tropical forest, or
desert can be created in every region to increase social and individual
awareness and experience of the major terrestrial ecosystems. The
skin structure of the dome is controlled pneumatically or electrostati-
cally so that the solar and earth radiation are adequately filtered in
order to maintain the right ecological conditions of temperature,
humidity, rainfall, and air circulation in a quasiclosed system.[1]

In circulating coined landscapes, minted and preserved by the environmental modulation of the architectural container, Navarro Baldeweg
presciently conceived architecture as an active medium—an economy—
of experiences. Yet, despite the artificiality of its circulating ecologies, the
project invested in an earthbound phenomenology as the fundamental
reservoir of human understanding. While, over the next thirty years, the
means for realizing such (ecological) experiences have become an increasingly sophisticated and theorized aspect of architectural production,
progressive architectural practice has severed the tether binding ecological experience to the replication of found natural conditions. In this
way, Navarro Baldeweg's project occupied a poignant threshold between
hitherto analogical and henceforth material conceptions of architectural
ecology.

The analogical origins of Navarro Baldeweg's project, produced while
in residence at Kepes's Center for Advanced Visual Studies at MIT, are
largely attributable to Kepes. Invested in the intertwining of the natural
and social sciences, in the fruitful legacy of nineteenth-century biological thought, and what he took to be the promising revival of this legacy in
the postwar period, Kepes drew seamless, organic analogies between the
self-regulating processes of the human body, cybernetic-computational
control, and the socioenvironmental corpus. Kepes asserted that the
potency of this thought for environmental regulation was the realization
of a "self-conscious evolution" effected "through social communication."[2]
"We can see the beginnings of broad ecological feedback machines," he
projected, "that sense our danger and work toward resolving the problem
of man's relations with his surrounding."[3] Kepes described environmental devastation as both an ecological *and* cultural concern, the loss of the

riches that art had timelessly plundered for sensible inspiration. Faced with this realization of the artist's loss of a stable foundation in nature—the groundless immersion in the shifting and often fickle currents of mass society—Kepes viewed art as a means of rendering intellectually transparent otherwise obfuscated processes of nature and culture. For Kepes, Navarro Baldeweg's project was exemplary of the artist's role; the artist was uniquely suited to mediate and control public sentiment because his work offered the potential of a sustainable, deeper, more sensory inculcation of ecological awareness than was possible through the elaboration of intellectual facts alone.

In this respect, Kepes was engaging a central dilemma of American progressivism, which had long struggled in its conception of agency with the tension between rationality and sentiment. The architectural historian Reinhold Martin has clearly explicated Kepes's central place in the engagement of postwar modern architecture and design with what he has called the "organizational complex": the interdisciplinary collaborations characteristic of the postwar American military-industrial complex; the imbrications of government, academia, corporations, and mass media that sought, through the extension and integration of networked systems, unbounded modes of control.[4] Yet it is the genealogy of the organizational complex in interwar American social science that sheds most light on the shifting fortunes of progressive architecture's environmental agency. The research institutes identified by Martin as the crux of the organizational complex can be seen as highly instrumentalized versions of those institutions developed in the interwar period, when philanthropic organizations embraced the rapidly professionalizing social sciences as the basis of an enlightened bureaucracy central to democratic governance. These quasi-academic, quasigovernmental, interdisciplinary research centers sought, through the objectivity of social science, to be neutral clearinghouses for essential regulatory information.

In the highly influential thought of the Chicago School of sociology—the dominant school of American and urban sociology in the middle decades of the twentieth century—this mediating role for the social sciences in progressive American democracy was explicitly cast in the terms of ecology. The seminal statement of the school, Ernest Burgess and Robert Park's *Introduction to the Science of Sociology* (1921), defined sociology as the discipline of "social control," the discipline of planning par excellence, transforming experience into knowledge in a progressive conception of human development as the "control over physical nature and eventually over man himself."[5] Coining the term *human ecology*, Park and Burgess conceived sociology as the nervous system of the social organism, modulating the fickle psychology of mass society. In *The City* (1925), the Chicago sociologists inaugurated an application of these ideas to American urbanism, taking the idea of "succession" from plant ecology—the transformation of an environment by an ecology of species that renders it habitable by a successive ecology of species—to assert a progressive transformation in the settlement patterns of American cities. To a significant degree, modeled on his earlier collaboration with pragmatist philosopher John Dewey, but also German thinkers such as Georg Simmel and Ferdinand Tönnies (also influential for modernist European architects), Park's sociology argued the central role of communication and mobility in the city—the heightened level of social contact and circulation of ideas—would transform a metropolis fragmented by the inherited alliances of ethnicity and class into a social field of liberated interest.[6]

In the halls of American academia in the late 1930s and 1940s, modernist architects and planners, such as the German émigré Walter Gropius, seeking to leverage his foothold in the United States, and his American acolyte Reginald Isaacs, engaged these progressive social scientists both directly and discursively. Kepes, himself an émigré, resident at László Moholy-Nagy's newly established Institute of Design (the New Bauhaus) in Chicago, was also thoroughly immersed in this social-scientific discourse. Yet to the extent that there was tension between these sympathetic architects and designers and the social-scientific American planning establishment, it concerned the agency of the artist and artistic form; the question of the relationship between rationality and aesthetics was by no means foreign to, nor reconciled by, the broader progressive discourse itself. Indeed, the midcentury lament, for the as-yet irreconcilable realms of thought and feeling, promulgated by the quintessential advocate of modernism, the Swiss architectural historian Sigfried Giedion, was consistent with progressive social scientists' contemporaneous desire to account for unenlightened and lingering communal sensibilities through more effective modes of instrumental communication. In the midcentury concern with a new monumentality, the civic center, the superblock, slum clearance, and social housing, it is possible to see the architectural corollary of this political-scientific project to create a rational environment, a society of conscious choice rather than inherited mores.

Yet the postwar instrumentalization of interwar progressivism radically transformed modern architecture's self-assumed benevolent objectivity. If interwar progressivism was buoyed by the Deweyan assertion of a prevailing social intelligence, the postwar period increasingly engaged a rationale of irrationality—advertising, mobilized prejudice, the political campaign, the cold war (total war)—as the means of social control. With the instantaneity of electronic communication, the emancipatory human ecology envisioned by the interwar social sciences metamorphosed into the totalizing media ecologies of the 1950s and 1960s. The institutional objectivity of a hitherto judicious progressivism was instrumentalized and desecularized as the pure immediacy of a social sensorium.

The deep crisis of architecture in this period can be attributed, in large part, to the discipline's ongoing engagement with this increasingly technologized, bureaucratized, and totalizing agency, exemplified by Kepes's vision of the artist as regulator of ecological perception. Indeed, Kepes's assertion of the centrality of the artist in ecological management—an implicit projection of modernist concerns with the industrial city onto the global environmental question—was born of an identification of new technological means. Kepes asserted "the artist had the opportunity to contribute to the creative shaping of the earth's surface on a grand scale," due to the new global perspective, the "new scale consciousness," afforded by technological achievements. Moreover, Kepes identified an architectural trend in keeping with the emphasis on systems and processes in science and the other arts, toward the liberating dematerialization of architectural form. Kepes held out the promise of a "light and transparent" architecture of "'thingless' events," an architecture that in its "flexible, mobile, transparent lightness," could "contribute significantly to man's liberation from fixed space enclosure that separated him from nature's wealth of events."[7] In short, like many architects at this time,

Kepes envisioned a formless, purely instrumental architecture of environmental immediacy.

For Kepes, Navarro Baldeweg's project rendered the ocean a frictionless clearinghouse of ecological information. The near transparency of the architectural medium and the indeterminacy of content in the photomontages stood for the promise of an instrumental, postmediated system: an envisioned immediacy between affect and effect, between the experience of natural landscapes and "ecological consciousness."[8]

Contemporary Material Ecologies

While the distributed, technological networks of the postwar Pax Americana promised the apotheosis of a humanistic social control, they instead gave rise to both the hypermediated and unmediated events of a nascent counterculture. By 1972, contrary to Kepes's commitment, perceptions of architecture's environmental efficacy were in full-blown crisis. With the dawning realization that the control of nature underpinning modernist theories of social progress had not been effected, there emerged an environmental activism contiguous with, but no longer encumbered by, the social, political, and economic episteme that formerly dominated environmental concerns. Therefore, at the very moment an increasingly global conception of environmental primacy was being forged, established modes of environmental planning and architectural agency were being discredited. Against the hegemony of modernism, a new generation of architects and planners sought out what amounted to largely incommensurable alternatives. While the postmodern period realized significant new modes of architectural efficacy and numerous material and organizational means of environmental control, these developments were often culturally regressive, environmentally detrimental in their isolated application, or focused more toward progressive sociocultural than ecological concerns.

Moreover, on the ground of the mediated second-nature created in the postwar period, the progressive ideal of a plastic society of mutual interest, born of an environmental commons, was instead fabricated in spectacular fashion as a commodified self-interest, manifest in expressive identity and the hyperreal ecology of experiences. Without fully eroding ghettos of ethnicity and class, the concluding decades of the American century laid out a second stratification articulated in the choice brands of politics and lifestyle. Deeply implicated within this landscape of identity and experience, ecological awareness and environmental ambivalence is increasingly affected through manners of shopping, appetites, fashion, and group affiliation.

Yet it is this plural field—an increasingly localized ecology of lifestyles—that constitutes the potential for a new, now disequilibrating, empiricism; a successive neoprogressivism that takes the environment *as such* as its medium, rather than the environment conceived as primarily an ethereal communicative mode.

Rather than seeking to subsume irrational sensibilities, to synthesize a universal consciousness as the basis of future ecological awareness and regulation, or presupposing the efficacy of globally integrated systems and agencies, this is an environmental movement of largely ad hoc projects, based on collectives cobbled together in recognition of the latent potential inherent within the qualitative differences frequently manifest in contingent conditions. This is a potential born in the specificities of local crises and opportunities, regional topographies and resources, and contingent political and institutional alignments; a potential latent in the legacy of modernism's functional division of architectural spaces, institutions, and geographical areas, and by the spatial and symbolic differentiations of late capitalism.

At its hitherto most efficacious, this new agency—chiefly operating under the rubric of landscape urbanism, but also apparent in certain temporary installations and speculative projects—precipitates action through interventions and images that fabricate ecologically productive environments as the mediating material moment of an active, albeit often highly regulated, cosmopolitan life. While these visions frequently leverage extant identities and sentiments in their engagement with the material contingencies of a locality, the progressive potential of this work is ultimately the cultivation of social, experiential, and physical difference as the ongoing catalyst for sustainable social and material ecologies. That is, this new architectural agency promises the fabrication of localized, qualitative difference as the sustaining potential of perpetually progressive socioecologies.

Perhaps the boldest theory of this kind was sketched out in MVRDV's Dutch Pavilion at Hannover's Expo 2000 in Germany (2000). Like Navarro Baldeweg, MVRDV also coined ecosystems, but rather than conveying natural values, the "artificial ecologies" stacked like pancakes in Hannover slip seamlessly between categories, never simply extant landscapes, but synthesized elements, moods, pleasures, productive sites, narratives, and associations.[9] [FIG. 03] Across and between the vertically stacked ecologies of the pavilion—Water, Rain, Forest, Oyster, Agriculture, Grotto—architecture and landscape were deeply implicated in a system that equally enacted both passive and active, environmental and social programs (from vapor cooling and conferences, to water purification and film projection). MVRDV embraced the potential that lies between highly differentiated ecologies, realizing this potential as flows of matter and energy in addition to its surreal programmatic possibilities.[10] [FIG. 04] Rather than affective symbolic feedback seeking to effect a unified environmental consciousness, the Dutch Pavilion enacted real environmental feedback—matter and energy generated in one part of the building reused in another—to proliferate new sensibilities. The juxtaposition of highly differentiated landscapes and functions intensified both efficiencies and qualities, as energy, vital materials, and people were cycled and recycled through the structure.

While the work circulated this manifold experience as "Dutchness," it was not the cumulative experience of varying landscapes that represented the national brand so much as the very constitution of these landscapes as a fabricated, experiential, and experimental system. The Netherlands was conceived less as an extant place and more as a theory of human habitation and cooperation for an emerging condition of ecological imperatives. "The Netherlands is a densely populated country combining a high standard of welfare with a great democratic tradition," the architects wrote of the project. "It could well be the prime example of a country that has always had to (and know how to) mould the environment to suit its will." Faced with the demographic and ecological realities of the planet, MVRDV thus asserts environmental agency as the precondition of contemporary progressivism, but a progressivism now conceived, not in terms of a single historical transformation, or universal, globally networked solutions, but in constructions that have—to

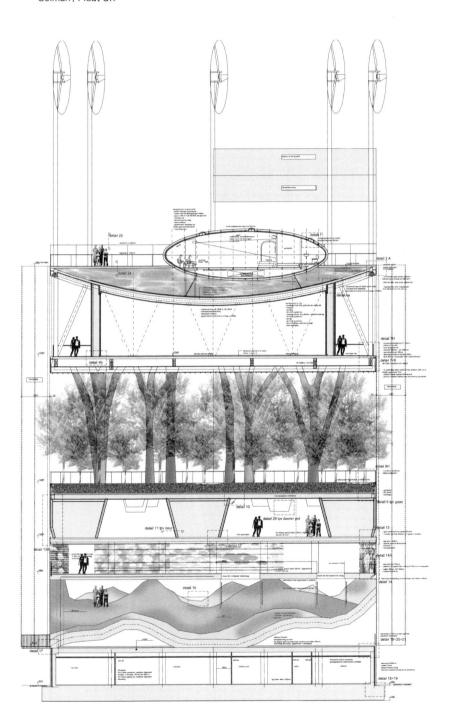

FIG. 03 Building section, MVRDV, Dutch Pavilion, Expo 2000, Hannover, Germany, 2000

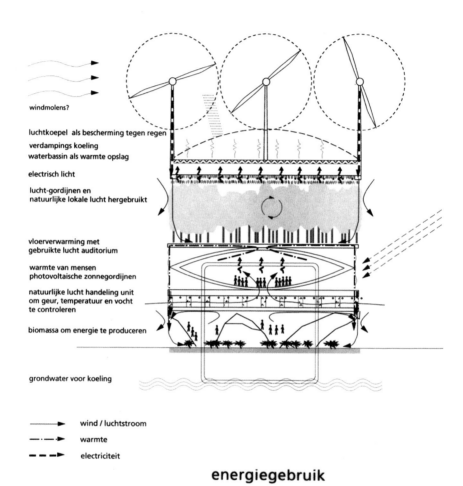

windmolens?

luchtkoepel als bescherming tegen regen
verdampings koeling
waterbassin als warmte opslag

electrisch licht

lucht-gordijnen en
natuurlijke lokale lucht hergebruikt

vloerverwarming met
gebruikte lucht auditorium

warmte van mensen
photovoltaische zonnegordijnen

natuurlijke lucht handeling unit
om geur, temperatuur en vocht
te controleren

biomassa om energie te produceren

grondwater voor koeling

→ wind / luchtstroom
—·—► warmte
— — —► electriciteit

energiegebruik

FIG. 04 Energy flow diagram, MVRDV, Dutch Pavilion, Expo 2000, Hannover, Germany, 2000

FIG. 05 Dutch Pavilion, MVRDV, Expo 2000, Hannover, Germany, 2000

cite their own descriptions—"the character of a happening" as well as a certain monumentality.[11] [FIG. 05]

Progressive Architectural Ecology

It is, above all, the artifice of this economy of experiences that constitutes both the ecological theory of the Dutch Pavilion and its implicit defense of the longstanding agency of the architectural project. Rather than seek to absolve society in global material and energy flows, the Dutch Pavilion suggests edifices that productively internalize and intensify human agency, thus realizing sustainable agency as a condition of socioenvironmental progress.

This desire for a sustained agency has led to a number of projects that countenance the edification of the city—and even, as MVRDV's consideration of the Dutch state shows, entire regions—as constituting a prospective progressivism. The Office for Metropolitan Architecture's (OMA's) prototype City in the Desert for the United Arab Emirates (2006), for example, proposes dense oases, with their consequent pleasures and efficiencies, as the very possibility of sustainability in a hostile climate, simply by drawing a line in the sand. In the face of unsustainable settlement and demographic realities, such projects propose precise loci as prerequisite to intensified differentiation and sustainable settlement. These projects suggest that only with a critical density or biomass can the qualitative differentiations necessary to both cultural proliferation and economic and ecological transformation be constituted; only by realizing this potential in fully architecturalized urban organs can a settlement's sustaining hinterland—its effective landscape footprint—be reduced. Moreover, these projects assert an ecological accountability; their economy registered in their very objecthood. This urban sovereignty becomes not the girdle of the qualitative expansion and differentiation of cultural and environmental ecologies, but its very precondition. Unlike the dematerialized instruments envisioned by Kepes, these projects are articulated precisely in their embrace of architecture, their assertion of form, and their defense of design.

Therefore, these projects implicitly claim the value of disciplinary architectural research—the critical need to cultivate architectural ecologies (not simply technical solutions)—as requisite to the realization of sustainable ecologies. The Dutch Pavilion owes its lineage to the quintessential modern diagram, Le Corbusier's Maison Dom-ino (1915), and its more recent successor, Rem Koolhaas's "1909 theorem" (1978), both of which conceived architecture as a machine for the reproduction of earthly potential. In particular, however, the Dutch Pavilion owes its lineage to Koolhaas's consideration of early-twentieth-century skyscrapers, which he lauded in *Delirious New York* (1978) for their "reproduction of the world," their craning for "communication with what remains of nature," but also, given the indeterminacy of program on each of their manifold floors, for their attenuation, if not sabotage, of planning.[12] Yet MVRDV's accomplishment in the Dutch Pavilion is to have reinvested this liberal architecture with environmental planning; not the soulless systematic planning typically associated with environmental engineering (although this competency is part of it), but the formal and material organization of landscape planning, historically—in figures such as Ebenezer Howard in Britain and the Olmsteds and Charles Eliot in the United States—at the very root of twentieth-century urban progressivism. In a sense, Koolhaas and OMA instigated this marriage in a project seminal for landscape urbanism, their competition entry for Parc de la Villette (Paris, 1982). OMA rotated the diagram of the liberal skyscraper from vertical to horizontal and laid it across the landscape to articulate parallel bands of programmatic difference. In the Dutch Pavilion, MVRDV stacked these landscapes back up, bringing the stuff of landscape along with it. In so doing, MVRDV internalized planning as a function of a hitherto liberal type, sacrificing a certain degree of freedom in realizing the efficacy of its environmental systems, and therefore architecturalizing the longstanding tension between liberalism and planning in a fundamentally new way.

It is precisely the cultivation of this tension within architectural parameters—a circumscription by design—that suggests this tension can extend rather than exhaust architectural agency. The proliferation of manifold architectural ecologies empirically relaxes or intensifies this tension. For example, if the Dutch Pavilion errs in a certain overdetermination of its constituent ecologies, the more recent approach of OMA's ecologically focused urban work preserves a certain distinction between more and less determined zones. One alternative to MVRDV's stacked landscape planning is OMA's Dubai Renaissance project in the United

Arab Emirates (2006), which conceptually rotates the nineteenth-century liberal metropolis to create a skyscraper of diverse "neighborhoods" and public "boulevards." Just as these neighborhoods float like islands in this city-scraper, so too the skyscraper itself is slotted into one of three floating, artificial islands, which, through their differentiated ecologies, fabricate recreational and material potentials. While the spaces within the skyscraper preserve a certain indeterminacy, the form and mechanics of the building and the ecological specificity of the islands seek to generate sustainable material and energy flows. Similarly, in their project for Penang City (Malaysia, 2004), OMA deliberately constructs a mixed-economy of determinate and indeterminate spaces, an archipelago of strictly delimited, functionally defined islands with highly differentiated landscapes and architectural typologies floating in a tropical "soup."

Increasingly, it is through such differentiated and proliferating artificial islands that the empirical negotiation of progressivism and its limits is being conceived for its material, social, economic, political, and environmental potential. Indeed, in developing material and cultural linkages between increasingly differentiated and circumscribed socioenvironments, modernist functionalism, late-modernist systematization, and the postmodern economy of experiences become politically tolerable and mutually supporting. Like Navarro Baldeweg's jars of preserves, we can conceive these islands as if they float on the empirical medium of the earth. Yet rather than conveying a singular effective currency, it's the critical distance and relationships between the divergent ecologies of these archipelagos—these island chains of signifiers—that now seems most important to value and cultivate.

NOTES

1. György Kepes, "The Artist's Role in Environmental Self-Regulation," in *Arts of the Environment*, ed. György Kepes (Henley, UK: Aidan Ellis, 1972), 192, punctuation altered.

2. Kepes, "Art and Ecological Consciousness," in *Arts of the Environment*, 4.

3. Kepes, "The Artist's Role," 167.

4. Reinhold Martin, *The Organizational Complex: Architecture, Media, and Corporate Space* (Cambridge, MA: MIT Press, 2003).

5. Robert E. Park and Ernest W. Burgess, *Introduction to the Science of Sociology* (1921; repr., Chicago: University of Chicago Press, 1969), 339.

6. Robert E. Park, Ernest W. Burgess, and Roderick D. McKenzie, *The City* (1925; repr., Chicago: University of Chicago Press, 1967).

7. Kepes, "Art and Ecological Consciousness," 10–11.

8. Ibid., 9.

9. Stan Allen, "Artificial Ecologies: the Work of MVRDV," *El Croquis* 86 (1997): 26–33.

10. I owe the insight of this sentence to John McMorrough.

11. MVRDV, "Dutch Pavilion for the Expo 2000," *El Croquis* 111 (2002): 40, 43.

12. Rem Koolhaas, *Delirious New York: A Retroactive Manifesto for Manhattan* (1978; repr., Rotterdam: 010 Publishers, 1994), 85.

Big Nature
Jane Amidon

Since the 1980s, the number of landscape projects predicated on environmental remediation has burgeoned. In particular, new metropolitan-scale parks are emerging from the residues of twentieth-century urban, industrial, and military operations, suggesting a broad array of regenerative strategies that successfully incorporate complex constituencies and contexts. This trajectory is expected to continue and increase exponentially, contributing to a recent factoid from the Federal Bureau of Labor Statistics: the demand for landscape architecture services in the United States will increase by up to sixteen percent in the next six years.[1] But if we look further ahead, this kind of work will soon be obsolete. When developed economies sufficiently clean up and phase away the collateral contamination of the industrial era, what then? How will we design the next generation of landscapes and, more importantly, what will be our postremediation motivations?

In landscape and related disciplines, close attention is already being paid to practices that preempt the need for remediation. For example, innovations in industrial ecology reimagine the historically destructive activities of resource extraction, refinement, production, distribution, and postuser consolidation as interdependent modes in which the output (waste) of one process is harnessed as the input (nutrient) for others. Dematerialization, decarbonization, and life-cycle design have gained traction as economically feasible, environmentally pragmatic, and culturally rewarded strategies. As the practice of landscape moves beyond reclamation, there is a proactive, rather than reactive, stance. The paradigm is shifting to "making" instead of "fixing." Sites are producers— living systems—linked to supply and demand networks that deal with food and water security, renewable energy, and climate change issues.[2]

Today, public interest in the landscape is increasingly geared toward a fusion of economic/social/environmental vitalization, such as Detroit's urban farm programs and Chicago's Green Alley Program. For example,

the Chicago Department of Transportation's Green Alley Program aims
to replace conventional surfaces with pervious, reflective, and recycled
pavements on 1,900 miles (3,057 kilometers) of urban alleyways that
cover 3,500 acres (14,164 square meters) of city land.[3] The project hopes
to improve storm water filtration, reduce heat-island effects, and comple-
ment the city's other landscape initiatives, such as planting street trees
and encouraging implementation of green roofs on municipal buildings.
Here the idea of public space has been enlarged to include amenities for
people *and* the environment.

Public lands have not undergone a paradigm shift this consequential
since the advent of the National Park Service one hundred years ago, when
the National Park Act of 1916 established the preservation of remote wilderness in its pristine state as a right of U.S. citizens. Then the movement
was in response to intensifying rates of land consumption at the dawn
of an era of technocracy; preservation would create a vast land bank for
future generations. Now a change in attitude takes advantage of emerging environmental technologies to once again realign our relationship to
nature. But this time, rather than passively protecting it in far-off places
of wilderness and leisure, we are actively building an enhanced nature
around our daily existence that fuels, filters, feeds, and otherwise fosters
healthier communities. Preemptive and productive, generative landscapes, such as carbon-dioxide-eating, biofuel-producing, algae farms,
or a public water garden that is part civil infrastructure (storm water
management), part civic park, establish novel priorities. [FIG. 01] Instead of
fencing off wilderness tracts (the unspoiled, "far" landscape as a prized,
geographical figure), or remediating postindustrial parcels at the urban
periphery (the imperiled, "close" landscape as reclaimed terrain), efforts
are coalescing around ecological innovation as a civic action: the entrepreneurial landscape, a "big" hybrid of environmental conditions and social
agendas.

Operative Ecology as a Problem and a Solution
Before considering the idea of Big Nature more closely, it is worthwhile to
briefly trace the preceding eras of preservation and remediation because
they created the discourse from which this generation's entrepreneurial
landscapes stem. It is important to note that operative ecologies have long

FIG. 01 Watercourse, PEG-OLA, Venice Lagoon Park competition entry, Venice, Italy, 2007

been at the heart of human settlement. Only during the machine age was working nature rigorously held apart from the civic realm. The notion of parks as oases offering escape from the pressures of the city is at odds with the shared landscapes of earlier millennia, which were nexuses of human effort (*technos*) and ecology (*oikos*). Although large-scale environmental systems played a role in the formation of most cities (water bodies for transit; landform for prospect and protection; geologic, plant, and animal communities for habitation and sustenance; etc.), throughout the nineteenth and twentieth centuries working landscapes (ecological media) were routinely out-competed by the notion of a sublime Nature. This allowed modernizing nations to consume natural resources with minimal guilt so long as a version of the pristine, "far" landscape was preserved. In this period, ecological media were understood as little more than utility (raw materials) or ideology (regional aestheticism such as philosopher Ralph Waldo Emerson's transcendentalism, or the Hudson River school landscape painters).

By the mid-twentieth century, ecology took on the role of industrial victim, its threatened state of health becoming a poster child for protectionism. A backlash set in; in the United States, the Environmental Protection Agency changed its regulation standards and influential figures such as landscape architect Ian McHarg fed the public's fear of naturocide with the publication of the seminal book *Design with Nature*.[4] Nearing the end of the century, it was clear both stances—all-out consumption versus guilt-driven protection—had served to distance ecological realism from intellectually and materially progressive landscape design practices.[5]

But, by the 1980s, there were signs the oppositional relationship of technos and oikos was beginning to soften. As reclamation became a pervasive project type in Europe and the United States, remediation turned out to be both a design task and a new public forum. Between the brackets of Richard Haag's Gas Works Park in Seattle, Washington (1975)—one of the first parks in the United States implemented on industrially contaminated grounds—and the High Line in New York City (Field Operations; Diller Scofidio + Renfro, 2009)—an adaptive reuse of an elevated rail line—three strategies characterized significant remediation practices:

Inhabiting

Exemplified by Latz + Partner's Landscape Park in Duisburg Nord, Ruhr Valley, Germany (2002). Common modes include: architectural/horticultural interventions within the armature of obsolete production/refinement processes; reconfiguration of contaminated grounds into a programmed plane; juxtaposition of "then" versus "now" as scenographic and narrative devices.

Transforming

Parc du Sausset, Michel and Claire Corajoud, Aulnay-sous-Bois, France (1993); the Shell Project, West 8, Eastern Scheldt Storm Surge Barrier, Zeeland, Netherlands (1990); and AMD & ART Park, Julie Bargmann, Stacy Levy, Robert Deason, and T. Allen Comp, Vintondale, Pennsylvania (1995), were three of the first, truly operational reclamation projects, each predicated upon instrumentalized ecology. The grounds transitioned over time: at the urban periphery, Sausset's fusion of urban park, forestry, and agricultural zones, progressed from a preliminary condition (installation), through maturation (sylvacultural management), to climax (harvest); the plateaus of the Shell Project storm surge islands weathered from one configured materiality (field of shells) to a second (dunes of sand); drainage within the acid mine discharge ponds of AMD & ART Park metabolized from one alchemic status (contaminated) to another (cleansed). For these and similar works, the land art movement of the 1960s and '70s offered a model for instability in the designed landscape: actions such as inundation, deposition, erosion, growth, and decay provided meta-phoric language as well as a morphological formalism that differentiated postmodernism in landscape from that in architecture and urbanism. Increasingly literal in response to physical environs, the dynamic configu-ration and aesthetics of performance revealed by these landscapes were derived from direct engagement with site process. Cycles of event and recovery were embraced and framed by design, not defended against. Site as a cultural realm began to align with site as environmental function.

Recalibrating

By the late 1990s, remediative landscapes—particularly those cast as mod-els for the twenty-first-century park, such as the proposal for Downsview Park in Toronto, Canada, by the Office for Metropolitan Architecture, Bruce Mau Design, and Inside Outside (2000)—increasingly found in ecological theory a paradigm for metasite processes and emergent programs.[6] [FIG. 02] The appropriation of ecological principles such as suc-cession, disturbance regimes, disequilibrium dynamics, and the adaptive cycle of communities allowed landscape to further wean itself from the allied fields of architectural and art theory. Like transformation projects, the schemes progress more-or-less linearly toward an altered state of materiality, but with fluid program and identity. Increasingly large and combinatory, signature works of this period—primarily public parks—are characterized by the phasing of ecological states through introduced maintenance protocols; most simply, there is no site plan. Multiple phases of material management—a geotemporal matrix—replace design as a spatioformal practice.

The cohort of practices which emerged in the era of remediation now stand to influence how we will shape and use entrepreneurial environ-ments. These designers remarried the *idea* of nature with the real thing (working ecologies), mending centuries of divorce. They deployed the eco-logical medium as a means to speculate with clever science long before the current civic-minded turn to living systems.

Big Nature: Productive and Seductive

Looking beyond the preservation and remediation eras, as an entrepre-neurial Big Nature becomes the go-to landscape, a looming question is:

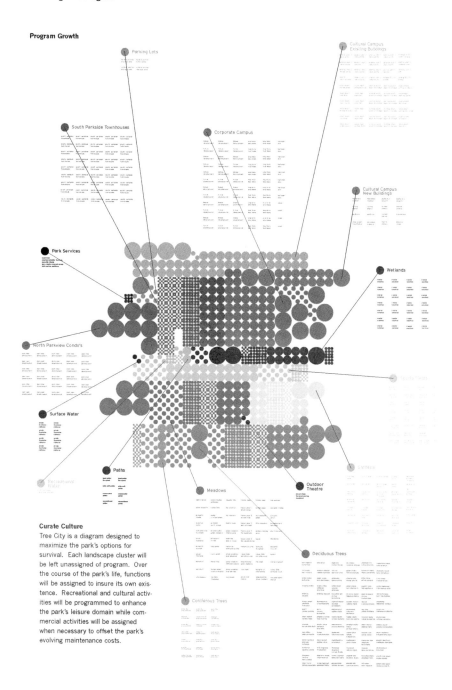

Program Growth

Curate Culture

Tree City is a diagram designed to maximize the park's options for survival. Each landscape cluster will be left unassigned of program. Over the course of the park's life, functions will be assigned to insure its own existence. Recreational and cultural activities will be programmed to enhance the park's leisure domain while commercial activities will be assigned when necessary to offset the park's evolving maintenance costs.

FIG. 02 Inside Outside, Bruce Mau Design, Petra Blaisse, and Rem Koolhaas/Office of Metropolitan Architecture with Oleson Worland Architects, competition proposal for Downsview Park, Toronto, Ontario, Canada, 2000

how will public space change? As new categories of technology remake our landscapes once again, how will we interact with the results? One aspect is clear: there is progress toward the performative matter of public space, toward reconciliation of nature and technology as an integrated application that is, by necessity, environmentally productive and socially seductive. And although critical theory has moved far beyond sustainability as a provocation, in many ways practice is just embarking on it. Productive and seductive, the nature of the next generation of landscapes is not docile and controlled, but governed by the potent interaction of natural and human forces.

The typological silhouette of landscape will continue to blur: shifting from an objectified spatial terrain to a subjective state, one substantiated by a capacity to produce localized benefits and experiential affect through active management of ecological media. For evidence of this shift in attitude toward site matter, compare the transformation of Byxbee Park, an obsolete landfill outside Palo Alto, California, by George Hargreaves/ Hargreaves Associates (1991), with Mapping the Ecotone, Ashley Scott Kelly and Rikako Wakabayashi's winning proposal for a new national park in the New York and New Jersey harbor in the Envisioning Gateways competition (2007). The earlier (sub/urban) park reconfigured topography and surface conditions to craft a new identity: rotting debris and contaminated soils were capped, then referenced, with small undulations planted with untended meadow grasses. [FIG. 03] Five site installations called attention to site dynamics, such as weather, light, and the passage of time. In comparison to signifying out-of-commission matter with static analogs,

FIG. 03 Reclaimed landscape, George Hargreaves/ Hargreaves Associates, Byxbee Park, Palo Alto, California, 1991

the Gateways proposal calls for zones of ecological tension (ecotones). [FIGS. 04-05] These ecotones reanimate salt marshes degraded by decades of fill and dredging and are scaled to integrate with Jamaica Bay. Microcosms of shifting habitats, program, and landforms are born from the intersection of dynamic material behaviors and armatures for public circulation. The project is environmental engineering writ large—a civil-civic typology that mixes high-rationalism with the romance of societal gain, echoing public works of the New Deal era. Formal organizations and aesthetic implications are not conceptual drivers but by-products of the living system—of splicing production techniques into existing urban site ecologies to amplify (positive) environmental effects.

In Mapping the Ecotone and other recent proposals, it is clear remediation of place has increasingly less to do with fixing environmental contamination and more with how we redefine our expectation of public spaces. In a handful of recent competitions and conferences, projects speak to the potential of cultivating living systems that are entrepreneurial hybrids of ecology, technology, and social agendas. Several common traits are apparent. The landscape tends to demonstrate one or more of the following conditions:

Interconnected

Entrepreneurial environments don't function as individual sites and material states but as pieces of a continuous, productive regional landscape—constellations that are not explicitly networked but share gravities.[7] For example, Hellenikon Metropolitan Park in Athens, Greece, by David Serero, Elena Fernandez, and the Office of Landscape Morphology (2004) creates a continuous, productive regional landscape that links urban fabric to the waterfront with topography, water, and vegetation corridors. [FIG. 06]

Multitasking

Globally, societal fixes for poverty, healthcare, and education are merging with environmental solutions; we can't solve one of these problems without paying attention to the others. One such example, Global Warming/ Local Freezing (2005), a proposal by Gross.Max for a nuclear-powered iceberg in a town square, suggests the exaggeration and displacement of

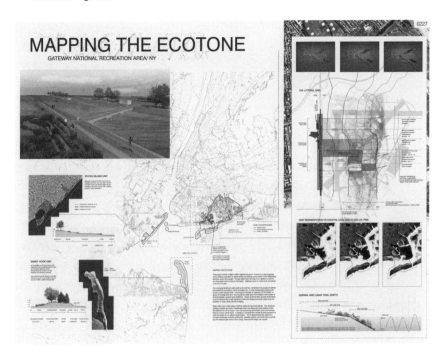

FIGS. 04-05 Mapping the Ecotone, Ashley Kelly and Rikako Wakabayashi, winning proposal for Envisioning Gateway competition, New Jersey, 2007

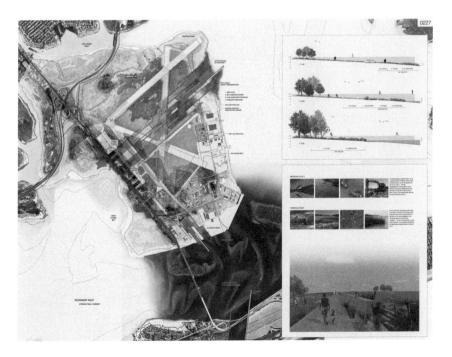

FIG. 06 Master plan, David Serero, Elena Fernandez, and the Office of Landscape Morphology, Hellenikon Metropolitan Park, Athens, Greece, 2004

nature's innate characteristics to gain public advocacy for the relatively abstract concept of climate change. Heightened material states (ice, steam, melting, freezing) enable productivity (lowered temperatures) and seduction (participation) by being demonstrative but not deterministic. [FIG. 07]

Consensual

At the heart of these landscapes is a symbiosis of ecology and technology that blurs distinctions between the natural and the artificial. From Geographic Information Systems (GIS) to Building Information Modeling (BIM), from hybrid super-plants to smart skins, pervasive info- and ecotechnology fuses buildings, landscapes, and cities into contiguous environments that are responsive and resilient. This suggests a dissolution of individual design pursuits; "landscape," "architecture," and "urbanism" are replaced with a new environmentalism that signals not merely semantic preference, but a shift away from the constraints of disciplinary autonomy. [FIG. 08]

Hurdles

At the same time, there are numerous hurdles to be crossed as these landscapes are implemented. First, in order to avoid the pitfalls of boutique ecology—the "crafty attempts by designers to get on the 'eco' bandwagon without linking the project to the messy and unpredictable dynamics of nature"—a productive *and* seductive Big Nature will need to test the real-time intersection of urban and natural systems.[8] Second, the modern public rarely warms to productive land uses, particularly in the United States. Ironically, for an economy founded upon land-based industry and agriculture, our preference tends strongly toward passive scenery as opposed to productive assemblies.

As preceding eras of change suggest, there is an image problem to be dealt with as we grapple with utility and accessibility in the entrepreneurial landscape of Big Nature. After the establishment of the national park system, it took the combined efforts of federal publicity programs plus the tourism, rail, and auto industries to galvanize the American public to visit their preserved wilderness (and its not-so-pristine boundaries, rife with commercial enterprise). Half a century ago, widely read books, such

FIG. 07 Global Warming/Local Freezing, Gross.Max, entry for the 6000 Miles Exhibition, Scotland, 2005

FIG. 08 Piazza Di Laguna
project, SLA, master plan and
landscape design; Henning
Larsen Architects, master plan
and building design; Autonome
Forme, building design;
Rambøll, engineering, Venice,
Italy, 2007

as Rachel Carson's *Silent Spring*, created demand for reclamation, but it took two more decades before we figured out how to combine remediation with cultural programming—in projects such as Gas Works Park.[9] Today, information and environmental technologies have the potential to virally increase awareness of ecological states, to link people, place, productivity, and performance. But people must comprehend and value the hybrid landscape of nature-technology, or it won't survive as a typology of public space. To promote itself across a gradient of cultural preferences, Big Nature will need to provide modes of physical and intellectual participation in addition to ecological production. Applied ecological media—the green, blue, and brown stuff—must function simultaneously as ideological mechanism and applied science long after *An Inconvenient Truth* fades from best-seller lists.[10]

Conclusion

For years I've asked my students to think deeply about the concept of nature—nature as both a cultural construct and a set of physical facts. To start, we use the familiar paradigm of first, second, and third nature: wilderness (nature alone), agriculture (nature + humanity), culture (nature + art, religion, leisure). I propose two more categories to students: a fourth nature of industry (nature + mechanization) and a fifth, postindustrial nature (reclamation). We conclude by asking, is there a sixth nature? What is next? There have been a range of responses, but the most common is a kind of green urbanism: nature as an ecometropolis of interwoven, sustainable systems. Excepting prefab ecocities—such as China's Dongtan Island project, designed by engineering–design firm Arup to be self-sufficient in water, food, and energy use, have a zero-carbon transit system, and 100 percent sustainable building construction—this is a relatively futuristic scenario. We will not be able to shed the constraints of our current urban infrastructures for generations to come; we have to make modifications from within. As priorities change, concepts of nature and, subsequently, strategies for land use evolve. Until recently, the missing link between the reclamation era (fifth nature) and authentically green cities (sixth nature) has been social motivation. We are just now coming to terms with the fact that our landscapes need to arouse desire in the public—desire to participate, desire to cultivate, desire to advocate.

A key to this rising awareness is the sense we are living in a time of recurring natural catastrophes; each successive hurricane, tsunami, wildfire, melting ice cap, and drought binds the social aspirations of first-, second-, and third-world economies into a common predicament. The "tragedy of the commons," old as human settlement, has grown exponentially since the industrial revolution. Loosely described, it concerns unfettered demand for finite natural resources: the benefits of exploitation accrue to select individuals or groups, while the costs are distributed, ultimately destroying the shared resource because no parties are responsible for its well-being. But in an essay in *Science* in 1968, University of California Professor of Biology Garrett Hardin pointed out: "In a still more embryonic state is our recognition of the evils of the commons in matters of pleasure."[11] Hardin introduced a moral component to choices about how and why we use natural resources. Today we are coming to recognize Hardin's insight at the macro scale. Our activities have tipped the balance and our lifestyles have become an endangered commodity. What was once a primarily economic and environmental equation is now a tragedy of the common(er). As climate change increases the severity of weather patterns, storm cycles, and seasonal extremes, survival of consumerist society is tied to a technological nature that is both beneficent (productive) and angry (destructive).

In short, the environment has become a social enterprise and society an environmental enterprise. As a trajectory of motivations, it is clear the ideological urge, and economic and environmental necessity to right our wrongs via remediation, provided a foundation for today's complex and preemptive socioecologies. If we examine current proposals and their roots in reclamation, there is progress toward a regional materialism: culturally and systemically healthy sites that awaken participants' perception of place and its processes. As productive ecologies are increasingly reintegrated within the civic realm, more individuals will participate in a Big Nature of live content that broadens the definition of social networking to include environmental matters. How will we respond? For now, the forecast is that the YouTube generation, accustomed to pervasive connectivity, information habitats, and unbridled individuation, will find in these dynamic landscapes fluid modes of participation and exchange, a means to sync with ambitious social and environmental identities.

Does this genre of work simply signal a revival of the second nature—the working landscape: an endemic (now technologically enhanced) environment we inhabit, tend, and depend upon for its functionality in a very real way? Or perhaps we are reaching toward new cultural terrain in which we are matter too. Our performance—how we consume, how we waste— is incontrovertibly connected to the state of the environment. We have always had a desirous relation to nature—whether agrarian or industrial, literary or aesthetic. As our technological culture accelerates toward entrepreneurial environments, bonding with Big Nature may come… well, naturally.

Recently, critic and landscape architect Richard Weller pointed out that "landscape architecture is yet to really have its own modernism, an ecological modernity, an ecology free of romanticism and aesthetics."[12] Because of their functionalism, we are tempted to understand these next landscapes as a kind of ecomodernism. But to flourish, they will need to appeal, if not to our sense of romance, at least to our sensibility about how decisions we make today impact the future. We are no longer innocent; contemporary culture is coming to grips with the Anthropocene epoch, a period that, Nobel Prize–winning chemist Paul Crutzen suggests, began in the late 1700s with the onslaught of fueled human activity.[13]

The onus of our new environmentalism includes a call for an advanced stewardship that is not just about protection or remediation, but an entrepreneurial redefinition of our relationship to nature.

NOTES

1. American Society of Landscape Architects, "Demand for Landscape Architecture Services Remains High: Many Firms Hiring in First Quarter 2008," February 11, 2008, www.asla.org/press/2008/release021208.html.

2. Liat Margolis and Alexander Robinson, *Living Systems: Innovative Materials and Technologies for Landscape Architecture* (Basel: Birkhäuser, 2007).

3. Chicago Department of Transportation, *The Chicago Green Alley Handbook: An Action Guide to Create a Greener, Environmentally Sustainable Chicago*, http://egov.cityofchicago.org/webportal/COCWebPortal/COC_EDITORIAL/GreenAlleyHandbook.pdf.

4. Ian McHarg, *Design with Nature* (Garden City, NY: American Museum of Natural History and the Natural History Press, 1969).

5. See Elizabeth K. Meyer, "The Post-Earth Day Conundrum," in *Environmentalism in Landscape Architecture*, ed. Michel Conan (Washington, DC: Dumbarton Oaks Research Library and Collection, 2000), 187–244.

6. Lance H. Gunderson and C. S. Holling, eds., *Panarchy: Understanding Transformations in Human and Natural Systems* (Washington, DC: Island Press, 2002).

7. See André Viljoen, ed., *Continuous Productive Urban Landscapes: Designing Urban Agriculture for Sustainable Cities* (Burlington, MA: Architectural Press, 2005).

8. William Thompson, "Boutique Ecologies," *Landscape Architecture Magazine*, April 10, 2006, 11.

9. Rachel Carson, *Silent Spring* (Boston: Houghton Mifflin, 1962).

10. Albert Gore, *An Inconvenient Truth: The Planetary Emergency of Global Warming and What We Can Do About It* (Emmaus, PA: Rodale Press, 2006).

11. Garrett Hardin, "The Tragedy of the Commons," *Science* 162 (December 13, 1968): 1243–48.

12. Richard Weller, "An Art of Instrumentality: Thinking Through Landscape Urbanism," in *The Landscape Urbanism Reader*, ed. Charles Waldheim (New York: Princeton Architectural Press, 2006), 69–85.

13. See Peter Schwartz, "We've Been Changing the Climate for Eons, and That's Reason for Hope," *Wired*, February 25, 2008, http://www.wired.com/science/planetearth/magazine/16-04/st_essay.

Garden for a Plant Collector, Glasgow
Bridget Baines and Eelco Hooftman of Gross.Max

Landscape Architecture as the skillful, accurate, and magnificent interplay of assembled vegetation under light....

Jean Des Esseintes, the illustrious protagonist of Joris-Karl Huysmans's exquisite, decadent novel *Against Nature* (1884), was a passionate collector of the most bizarre, hideous, and monstrous plants from around the world. Whilst inspecting his collection of natural flowers—which actually did look like fake ones—Des Esseintes enthusiastically proclaimed: "Without a shadow of a doubt, the horticulturists are the only true artists left to us nowadays...."

The Garden for a Plant Collector is located in Art Park (Bellahouston Park), Glasgow, in close proximity to Charles Rennie Mackintosh's House for an Art Lover (1901). A minimal glasshouse composed of layers of high performance luminous glass displays a surreal rockery of lush ferns and carnivorous plants. The glasshouse can be interpreted as a contemporary cabinet of curiosities paying tribute to the wonders of nature.

FIG. 01 Conceptual proposal, Gross.Max, Garden for a Plant Collector, Glasgow, Scotland, 2005

FIGS. 02-05 Cultivation environment,
Gross.Max, Garden for a Plant Collector,
Glasgow, Scotland, 2005

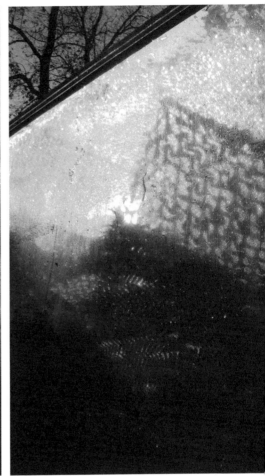

Regenerative Landscapes—Remediating Places

Anneliese Latz of Latz + Partner

Aesthetic Demands in Ecological Design

Within the last few years, especially in Europe, new public spaces have been developed by converting places of former industrial production and space-dominating infrastructure systems. This process is unthinkable without the development of specific ecological strategies. It must be our urgent concern to realize these strategies through design.

Landscape Park, Duisburg Nord: a Metamorphosis

One of Latz + Partner's biggest tasks of the last fifteen years has certainly been the redevelopment of the former Thyssen steelworks in Duisburg. This transformation of 568 acres (230 hectares) of industrial wasteland into a new urban landscape has had a strong economic and social impact on the depressed neighborhoods in the immediate vicinity.

In Duisburg we were given the chance to deal with ecological, functional, and social demands characteristic of large and densely populated agglomerations. Disused, formerly productive land opened the prospect of creating an oasis within an urban desert: a new landscape with remarkable climatic effects and extensive possibilities for both short- and long-term recreation and cultural activities.

Through careful intervention, creating new connotations, we maintained the site's industrial heritage, but made it accessible and usable in new ways. [FIG. 01] This was accomplished by managing the more than one hundred species of so-called neophytes that had been growing on slag and coal dust since the plant's closing, and by introducing plant typologies like chestnut or cherries, to create places for public use amidst the gigantic dinosaurs of the industrial era.

The project is concerned with the traditional, cultural term "garden"— a garden where we work or whose stillness and beauty we enjoy in contemplation. And it concerns the idea of a landscape, where instead of mountaintops, the man-made mountain ranges serve as landmarks

FIG. 01 Redevelopment of the former Thyssen Steelworks, Latz + Partner, Landscape Park, Duisburg Nord, Ruhr Valley, Germany, 1990–2002

within the chaotic urban fabric. On the other hand, their peaks create an aesthetic and visual demarcation of space, which had never before seemed possible in such areas.

We learned this site would not become a park in the traditional sense—not easy to survey, not clearly arranged, not recognizable as a whole. By using analytic methods we realized it is not necessary to impose a new order upon this chaos, and instead developed a system that makes it comprehensible. Following the structural parameters of the site, the individual systems in the park operate independently, connecting only at certain points through specific visual, functional, or merely symbolic linking elements. The "railway park" with its elevated promenades forms the highest level; the "water park" forms the lowest. Both run like ribbons through the site, rendering the otherwise chaotic area legible through their geometries. We learned that railway lines not only connect all the abandoned industrial sites, they also form the only continuous links within the park itself; they extend deep into the living and working areas of the surrounding city allowing the park to appear much larger than it is in reality. In particular, the railway bridges establish a coherence across the site which would not have been possible otherwise. We discovered the spectacular form of the large "rail-harp," a gravity system for the delivery of mass-produced goods employing a dozen or more tracks on different levels. Now it is experienced as a landscape of mountains and canyons, its gigantic dimensions conceivable only from the blast furnace observation platform.

The rail tracks end at storage bunkers, formerly filled with ore, coke, lime, slag, and semirefined products. A long footbridge was built above these bunkers as a place from which to view the bunker interiors that have been gradually transformed into gardens. Visitors can walk from a lower level into these enclosed spaces where vegetation prevails. From here the railway park is perceived as a second layer of information running overhead. [FIG. 02]

Another elevated walkway allows views into the dark "caves" of a second bunker plant adjacent to the blast furnaces and the hot blast stoves, which still awaits transformation. A system of paths, ramps, footbridges, and tunnels crisscrosses this labyrinthine structure, whose intimidating heaviness and mysterious darkness contrast with the brightness and beauty of other areas, effects achieved by very simple means: vegetation.

FIG. 02 An elevated footbridge provides views into former storage bunkers, Latz + Partner, Landscape Park, Duisburg Nord, Ruhr Valley, Germany, 1990–2002

FIG. 03 The "Old Emscher," Latz + Partner, Landscape Park, Duisburg Nord, Ruhr Valley, Germany, 1990–2002

One of the biggest ecological tasks was to create a new water system and new rainwater management strategy. In the bourgeois world, nature has been cultivated in contrast to technology. In an ecologically or sustainably oriented world, nature and technology have to present themselves homogeneously or even identically. This is the aim of the "water park."

Natural water no longer exists on the site; the upper zone of saturation, that is the upper part of the ground water aquifer, is heavily contaminated. The "Old Emscher," a former tributary of the Rhine, once an open wastewater canal carrying untreated sewage, crosses the park from east to west. The wastewater is now carried underground within a 11.48-feet-diameter (3.5-meter-diameter) main, sealed by a layer of clay, which collects runoff from the buildings, bunkers, and former cooling ponds. The cross-section of the old open sewer was used as the basis for the new clean-water system, in order to avoid contact with the polluted ground. [FIG. 03]

For the new clean-water system, rainwater is collected and directed to the new canal. It flows in open rivulets and through the existing overhead pipe systems, and then falls into the former cooling ponds, becoming enriched by oxygen in the process. The basins were cleaned by the members of a diving club who used to train in the deep "caves" of the former charge bunkers. Now, water lilies and iris bloom in pure water, and fish and dragonflies live in a new biotope. [FIG. 04] Former settling tanks have been cleaned and cleared of five hundred tons of arsenic mud (which was squeezed out of the tanks and deposited into old mines); and now, supplied with clear water, they provide a reservoir for the new water system. The old gasometer was filled with 32,000 cubic yards (25,000 cubic meters)

FIG. 04 Rainwater collects and oxygenizes in former cooling ponds, Latz + Partner, Landscape Park, Duisburg Nord, Ruhr Valley, Germany, 1990–2002

FIG. 05 The windwheel pumps water from the canal through the gardens, Latz + Partner, Landscape Park, Duisburg Nord, Ruhr Valley, Germany, 1990–2002

of water. Today it contains an underwater world for diving classes and public events.

The system of open and visible "water paths" leads through the blast furnace site towards the new canal. The collecting rivulets flow into the clean watercourse where platforms with seating lure visitors, and small islands are colonized by flora and fauna. A spectacular wind-driven oxygenation system was set up in the mill tower of the former sintering plant. The windmill has the biggest multiblade rotor in the world, with a diameter of 52.48 feet (16 meters). Water is pumped from the canal through an Archimedes screw and falls from several points after making its way through the gardens. [FIG. 05]

The water channel, like the whole water system, is an artifact that aims to restore natural processes in an environment of devastation and distortion. These processes are governed by the rules of ecology, but they are initiated and maintained with technology. Man uses this artifact as a symbol for nature, but remains in charge of the process. The system is at one and the same time entirely natural and entirely artificial.

We sought strategies for solving the problems posed by the pollution that was present, to varying degrees, in different parts of the park. We disposed of heavily polluted demolition waste on the site itself and built new, usable layers on top of it. Within the bunker site, for example,

FIG. 06 Piazza Metallica, Latz + Partner, Landscape Park, Duisburg Nord, Ruhr Valley, Germany, 1990–2002

FIG. 07 Gardens in the former sintering plant with industrial artifacts in the background, Latz + Partner, Landscape Park, Duisburg Nord, Ruhr Valley, Germany, 1990–2002

roof gardens cover the poisonous material which was removed from the surroundings and is now buried deep underneath. We used a surface material rich in lime with a high pH-value for the road system in order to encourage an already occurring process: slags, also of high pH-value, are capable of immobilizing heavy metals. In the area of the former cokery, we allowed for the gradual emission of small amounts of gas over the course of several generations, which would lead to a corresponding reduction in contamination. The contamination level permits limited uses such as cycling and walking. We recycled minimally polluted demolition waste for use as new plant substrates. We selected species that thrive in these soils without imported topsoil. Recycled bricks and concrete were ground for new construction material and recycled steel was used for new walkways and stairs.

Situated at the core of the former blast furnace plant, the Piazza Metallica symbolizes the metamorphosis of the hard and rugged industrial structure into a public space. Forty-nine cast-iron plates, once the lining of casting molds, were installed in the middle of the selected space. Unique forms of erosion caused by molten ore mark the surface of the plates. Cleaned of ashes and casting sediments, the plates reveal their subtle patterns and the process of their formation—becoming, in a sense, a symbol for nature. [FIG. 06]

Even though they have existed for some time, seen in a new way, the rational neutrality of the remains of industrial production becomes a semantic quality. [FIG. 07]

Studio 804

Dan Rockhill and
Jenny Kenne
Kivett of Studio
804

Studio 804—which takes its name from the final design studio within the graduate architecture program at the University of Kansas—compresses every aspect of a design-build practice into an intensive five-month experience. As a not-for-profit corporation, associated with the university but funded independently, the studio begins each year with nothing but the bank balance left by the previous graduating class and ends with a completed building, a satisfied client, and an invaluable learning experience. In the twelve years since the studio began, its focus has progressed from small-scale projects to creating affordable housing for the city of Lawrence, Kansas, to the point where students design, build, and install prefabricated homes for entry-level buyers in Kansas City. This experience paved the way for the studio's first commercial building, which achieved the U.S. Green Building Council's Leadership in Energy and Environmental Design (LEED) Platinum rating.

Modular Homes

Studio 804 offers a truly comprehensive experience, where students work not only with clients, neighborhood associations, and community development corporations (CDCs), but with building codes, structural engineers, inspectors, tradespeople, and real estate agents. Studio 804 helps students experience the complexities of building for the contemporary marketplace, preparing them for issues they'll confront as young professionals. The students find independent funding for each project, which enables a broad engagement with clients.

Since 2004, Studio 804 has produced modular, prefabricated homes for urban infill lots in Kansas City. By its very nature, prefabrication allows for flexibility in the process of design and construction. Delays due to inclement weather are avoided and the builder is able to use more efficient means to create a precision home. Additionally, the homeowner is given the opportunity for a customized yet affordable home. [FIGS. 01-04]

FIG. 01 Construction of Modular 1, Studio 804, Kansas City, Kansas, 2004
FIG. 02 Transportation of Modular 1, Studio 804, Kansas City, Kansas, 2005

The homes are designed and built in an off-campus warehouse and trucked to their sites. Originally, five site-built houses were erected in Lawrence, where the university is located. Shifting the focus to Kansas City delivered a number of benefits. The change provided much-needed housing stock for poor, underserved neighborhoods in which property values have remained depressed for decades. It connected Studio 804 with CDCs that were interested in modernist housing typologies that can attract the urban-hipster homesteader, the market that will form the bed-rock of the city's future. And it allowed Studio 804 to enter into contracts that provide tight, yet workable, budgets; amounts that challenge students to become better architects. Best of all, working in Kansas City has gener-ated gratifying results: the CDCs have sold many prefab homes to owners *before* they have left the warehouse.

Greensburg, Kansas

In 2008, the studio looked beyond Kansas City after one of the largest recorded tornados in history destroyed the town of Greensburg, Kansas. [FIG. 05] Determined to rebuild, the city was challenged by Kansas Governor Kathleen Sebelius to redevelop as a sustainable city. This meant the city had to adopt unprecedented regulations to make all publicly funded buildings LEED Platinum, at a time when there were none in the state.

Through partnership with the 5.4.7 Arts Center, a not-for-profit organization named for the date of the tornado, Studio 804 committed to supporting this goal by constructing the first LEED Platinum building in Kansas, and the first ever to be designed and built by students. [FIG. 06]

FIG. 03 Modular 1, Studio 804, Kansas City, Kansas, 2004

FIG. 04 Modular 2, Studio 804, Kansas City, Kansas, 2005

FIG. 05 Aftermath of an F5 tornado, Greensburg, Kansas, 2007

FIG. 06 Assembly of the 5.4.7 Arts Center, Studio 804, Greensburg, Kansas, 2008

FIG. 07 5.4.7 Arts Center, Studio 804, Greensburg, Kansas, 2008

The City of Greensburg turned funding concerns over to the art center and the studio. Studio 804 accepted this, knowing that without financial support they could not develop the project, and the studio took on all initial costs with the agreement that expenses would be paid back by the 5.4.7 Arts Center. The art center emerged as a 1,600-square-foot (150-square-meter) building, prefabricated in Lawrence, trucked to Greensburg, and set on a full basement.

The Studio 804 process has been consistent for all projects: beginning with a two-week design *charrette*—usually before a site has been identified—each student develops and presents a three-dimensional model. Within a few days, designs with similar characteristics are clustered, and these groups of students work to refine ideas that are ultimately combined into a single scheme. Construction documents are completed next and, typically, a building permit is acquired by the end of the month. That leaves students two months to physically construct the building in the warehouse, and six weeks for site and finishing work after the prefab modules have been moved and assembled.

The entire building is finished, inside and out, in the warehouse. Prefabrication imposes discipline on both the design and construction processes. The immutable restrictions imposed by issues such as the size of the warehouse door, the length and width of the flatbed truck, and the dimensions of the infill lot leave little room for argument and help to focus the students' abilities. [FIG. 07]

Built as a sustainable prototype, the 5.4.7 Arts Center implements passive and active strategies to reduce the overall heating and cooling load on the building. It incorporates sustainable materials as frequently as possible, including wood salvaged from the retired Sunflower Army Ammunition Plant, located between Lawrence and Kansas City. Established in 1941 as one of the world's largest powder and propellant plants, it is now excess federal property. Through the development company Sunflower Redevelopment, the property is being redeployed over time back into the public sector. Studio 804 secured the right to harvest structurally sound lumber from more than one thousand retired ammunition buildings, eliminating the need to use new lumber.

Cross ventilation and adequate shading on the building's broad south exposure keep the space from overheating in summer, while the concrete floor absorbs the sun in winter, helping to warm the space in the evening. Although passive attributes can provide for the majority of thermal comfort within the building, a forced-air system is still needed. Here, a geothermal heat pump is used instead of a conventional source, which, in conjunction with active collection systems, will attempt to negate energy use from the grid. Three horizontal-wind-axis turbines generate half of the necessary power for a typical, small commercial building. The Greensburg area is ideal for wind turbines: the prevailing southerly wind reaches an annual average speed of ten to twelve miles per hour (sixteen to nineteen kilometers per hour). The other half of the active system is dependent on a photovoltaic array, mounted on the roof and angled to provide maximum output.

The extensive site work included high fly-ash concrete for the plinth and sidewalks, a water reclamation system, and native grass. The recycling efforts encompassed both the materials used for construction of the building and managing on-site construction waste. The interiors incorporated water-saving, low-flow faucets and low-level volatile organic compound (VOC) adhesives and paints.

The design of the plinth was deliberate in its attempt to engage the public in a very active way. As the first permanent community building rebuilt in the town, it was important that it serve many functions, and this was accomplished by encouraging interaction between the building and its users. As a result, the art gallery acts as a space for meetings, parties, picnics, art classes, and lectures; it is transformed into the town theater on the weekends with movies on the lawn. This accessibility coupled with the building's downtown location has helped to reestablish Greensburg as a tourist destination point, drawing in curious visitors from states away.

The benefits of engaging students in a design-build process are incalculable. Studio 804 students learn to be responsible for everything. Most of all, they learn the value of working and communicating with others to achieve a common goal.

Dongtan Eco City

Arup

Arup was contracted in 2005 by the Shanghai Industrial Investment Corporation (SIIC) to design and plan Dongtan, an ecocity on Chongming Island close to Shanghai. Compared to business-as-usual urban development, ecocities deliver significant and measurable environmental, social, and economic gains. They demonstrate greater energy efficiency, better land usage, reduced resource consumption, and reduced emissions. To be truly sustainable, a city must not only be environmentally sustainable, but socially, economically, and culturally sustainable, too.

The Dongtan site, located at the eastern end of Chongming Island, is 21,000 acres (86 square kilometers). By 2050, SIIC hopes to accommodate up to 500,000 people on around 7,400 acres (30 square kilometers).

The master plan for Dongtan ensures the city will produce sufficient electricity and heat for its own use, entirely from renewable sources, including: a combined heat and power (CHP) plant that runs on biomass; a wind farm; biogas extracted from municipal solid waste and sewage; photovoltaic cells and micro wind turbines on individual buildings.

Energy demand will be substantially lower than comparable conventional cities due to the high performance of buildings and a zero-emission transport zone within the city. All housing is designed to be within a seven-minute walk of public transport, and have easy access to social infrastructure, such as hospitals, schools, and employment. Public transport will be powered by battery or fuel cells.

The Dongtan plan envisions the use of organic farming methods to grow food for the inhabitants of the city, where nutrients and soil conditioning will be used together with processed city waste. The development of techniques that increase the organic production of vegetable crops means that the area should remain as productive with reduced agricultural land as before the city was built.

FIGS. 01-02 Dongtan Eco City master plan, Arup, Dongtan Eco City, Chongming Island, Shanghai, China, 2005

All waste in the city will be collected and segregated at the source. Waste is considered to be a resource and most of the city's waste will be recycled with organic waste used as biomass for energy production. There will be no landfill in the city and sewage will be processed for energy recovery, irrigation, and composting.

The site is adjacent to a wetland of international importance for wildlife and migrating birds. The delicate nature of the wetland is one of the driving factors of the city's design. By returning agricultural land to a wetland state, the existing wetlands will be enhanced, creating a "buffer zone" between the city and the mudflats; at its narrowest point,

this "buffer-zone" will be 2.2 miles (3.5 kilometers) wide. Only around 40 percent of the land area of the Dongtan site will be developed as urban areas, and the city is designed to prevent pollutants (light, sound, emissions, and water discharges) from reaching the wetland.

The Dongtan plan incorporates many traditional Chinese design features to create a modern ecocity that is characteristically Chinese.

Toward an Ecological Building Envelope: Research, Design, and Innovation

Stephen Kieran, James Timberlake, and Roderick Bates of KieranTimberlake

KieranTimberlake has developed a series of environmentally responsive building envelopes driven by a deeply engrained research methodology. These envelopes create new expectations for how building facades can function, proving they should not just provide insulation and protection from the elements, but offer the potential to actively regulate the building environment.

Research, Design, and Innovation

We are committed to the process of innovation and strive to use research as a tool to integrate design and performance. Research is the most effective way to make a truly performance-based architecture that verifies environmental objectives. The aesthetic strength of our architecture is the result of our efforts to understand and assume responsibility for the environmental consequences of our buildings through research, design, and performance.

At the first stage of research for each project, we systematically and comprehensively explore the environmental context. This analysis identifies "opportunities" around which research may be applied and solutions developed. Social considerations imposed by both the client and the larger regional context, are also identified.

In the second stage, we use past-project precedents to address the opportunities identified by the site analysis. We are one of few architecture firms in the United States certified for the research, management, and delivery of architectural services by the International Organization for Standardization (ISO).[1] Our ISO process requires us to not only plan and perform work, but to monitor and learn from it. Inherent to the ISO system is a method of documentation, which provides a knowledge database of past research we can continue to draw upon.

The site-specific nature of architecture means many opportunities are likely to be unique. Prior research is used for inspiration and extension.

We often employ technologies transferred from other industries. Rather than providing a systemic path toward a solution, however, technology transfer requires meshing systems of disparate origin to address unique problems. Since we need to demonstrate the viability of a system or product before it is implemented, we explore ideas through mockups and computer models, and vet them against past experience, cost considerations, and expert advice. These efforts serve to refine the technology and ensure foreseeable contingencies are taken into account.

After design and construction, postoccupancy analysis helps determine if the technology achieves the desired performance, durability, and maintenance requirements. Methods for conducting this analysis include user interviews, site inspections, and the deployment of monitoring technology, such as temperature and airspeed sensors. This information tells us if in situ modifications are needed to optimize function and inform subsequent designs.

The countless lessons uncovered in the monitoring process allow us to learn and improve. To ensure this information is captured, the many small manipulations, discoveries, and monitoring data are recorded and shared within the firm through research documents, presentations, online wikis, and a blog. This closes the innovation loop, priming the cycle for the next project and its unique site opportunities. We have used the innovation cycle to develop various architectural systems, but the exploration discussed herein focuses exclusively on the development of high-performance facades.

SmartWrap

One of our more speculative projects provided much of the framework for our overall research agenda. The motivation for the development of SmartWrap—our trademarked envelope system—came from the desire to create a building skin that can generate energy, control climate, and provide lighting and information display on a single printed substrate. We designed a pavilion to exhibit the material and explain the concept in its architectural and artistic context—to describe its various components, and to demonstrate the transfer technologies upon which SmartWrap is based. The pavilion was first displayed as the inaugural Solos exhibit at the Cooper-Hewitt National Design Museum in New York (2003), and later

FIG. 01 SmartWrap demonstration, KieranTimberlake, Pavilion, the Cooper-Hewitt
National Design Museum, New York, 2003

traveled to Philadelphia, San Francisco, and the Vitra Design Museum
in Weil am Rhein, Germany. [FIG. 01]

To develop the material, we pursued emerging systems, including
organic light-emitting diode (OLED) displays; phase-change materials;
organic photovoltaics; print circuitry; heating elements; and a polyeth-
ylene-terephthalate (PET) substrate upon which the technology could be
printed. We used aluminum framing by Bosch Rexroth to create a structure for the material. After developing strategies to address the project
requirements, we analyzed and tested those strategies.

As an exercise in technology transfer, the key to SmartWrap was
seeking out technology producers to serve as feasibility experts. While
both the PET and the Bosch Rexroth framing had a proven track record
and required minimal research, other components, such as organic LED
technology and phase-change materials, were in their early stages of
development. Since our research found no currently developed system
for printing onto a substrate, we collaborated with DuPont and ILC Dover
to engineer and fabricate a working prototype. While the circuitry was
printed, ultimately some systems had to be adhered and sewn to
the SmartWrap. [FIG. 02]

FIG. 02 SmartWrap components, KieranTimberlake, Pavilion, New York, 2003

Cellophane House

The SmartWrap project, though experimental, was based on anticipated technology; the actual execution mattered less than the intention.
Components and partnerships from this project have been retained in
more recent projects, most notably in Cellophane House, an off-site-
fabricated dwelling, commissioned by the Museum of Modern Art in New
York for the exhibition Home Delivery: Fabricating the Modern Dwelling
(2008).[2] By reusing the Bosch Rexroth aluminum framing system and the
SmartWrap technology, which had benefited from five years of development since it was first exhibited, we were able to move beyond concept
and innovation to focus on refinement and feasibility. [FIG. 03]

Translucent or transparent materials were used for the walls, floors,
and roof of this five-story, braced-aluminum-frame structure. Cellophane
House is enclosed with a next-generation, thin-film SmartWrap skin
which, while visually engaging, also harvests energy from the sun through
integrated photovoltaic panels, and channels it through printed copper leads to a meter in the mechanical room. A second interior skin is
laminated with 3M ultraviolet film, allowing daylight to enter and dif-
fuse throughout the living spaces, while deflecting solar gain from the
interior space. Meanwhile, a passive ventilation system traps heat in
the winter, and vents it in the summer. These combined elements form
a double-skin wall that provides weather protection and contributes to

FIG. 03 Cellophane House, KieranTimberlake, Home Delivery: Fabricating the Modern Dwelling exhibition, the Museum of Modern Art, New York, 2008 © Peter Aaron/Esto

energy independence. [FIG. 04] To meet the challenge of balancing climate and thermal comfort in an enclosed PET structure without traditional insulation, we sought solutions in our previous experience with vented, double-skin facades. To counter the anticipated heat from New York summers, passive exhaust louvers facilitate a natural-venting, thermal-stack effect within the wall panels, while active ventilation around the bathroom cores ventilates the interior rooms.

To develop the next generation of SmartWrap, we had to verify that certain technologies, unavailable five years earlier, had been sufficiently developed. Some components were now available, while other systems were not yet ready for integration. Once we ascertained the possibilities, we formed partnerships with the firms providing expertise in these emerging fields, including PowerFilm, 3M, and DuPont.

Printed photovoltaics, one of the primary components we sought to use, were on the cusp of commercial development, but not yet ready for integration. By using commercially available, thin-film solar panels, affixed to the PET within the vented cavity of the wall panels, we were able to demonstrate the highest level of current development.

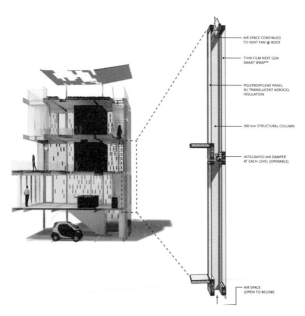

FIG. 04 Facade detail, KieranTimberlake, Cellophane House, Home Delivery exhibition, the Museum of Modern Art, New York, 2008

FIG. 05 Interior, Cellophane House, KieranTimberlake, Home Delivery exhibition, the Museum of Modern Art, New York, 2008 © Peter Aaron/Esto

When analysis indicated this vented wall would not be sufficient to maintain thermal comfort, an infrared-blocking film by 3M was chosen for its ability to shield the interior from solar radiation with minimal visual disruption. We were using Bosch Rexroth aluminum framing as the support structure for tensioned PET for the first time, and a full-size mockup revealed a significant deflection. This required a redesign using more and stronger aluminum units.

There will be significant, postconstruction analysis to evaluate the effectiveness of the venting facade involving the measurement of exterior, interior, and wall cavity temperatures. As a new technology with limited field-generated performance data, the roof-mounted, photovoltaic-integrated panels will be evaluated to determine power generation relative to deployment costs. Analysis is also being undertaken to help determine if the materials and systems lend themselves to reuse and recycling. All of the information will be used to improve the facade system, bringing it closer to commercial viability. [FIG. 05]

Loblolly House

At the Loblolly House (2006), a residence on the Chesapeake Bay in Maryland, we advanced our research into active facades. The waterfront house has free-flowing natural ventilation and an open view to the west.

FIG. 06
Loblolly House,
KieranTimberlake,
Chesapeake Bay,
Maryland, 2007
© Peter Aaron/Esto

[FIG. 06] The need for views called for an adaptive, permeable facade, while the short construction schedule required the use of existing technology.

The resulting design created an envelope through accordion-style folding glass walls by NanaWall as the interior wall, coupled with acrylic-clad hangar doors for the exterior envelope. Although we used off-the-shelf technology, our new composite active facade was a simple, effective, and low-cost solution. Cost made the use of Nanogel—an insulating powder that allows 20 percent light transfer—in the acrylic panels unfeasible. Although anticipated thermal performance was somewhat reduced, we found forgoing Nanogel to still be an environmentally effective, less-costly means of maintaining the desired aesthetic.

The exterior-mounted acrylic louvers serve as an adjustable sunshade and storm screen. They also trap the radiant heat that forms in the cavity when both layers are closed, providing thermal insulation. Although the cavity is not vented into the house, the trapped hot air limits diffusion of heat from the interior by reducing the temperature differential between interior and exterior air. When cooling is required, the louvers rotate perpendicular to the structure and the accordion doors fold back. This opens the western facade and transforms it into a screen allowing offshore breezes to flow through the house.

Unlike the extensive efforts required to prove the thermal characteristics of active facades in our larger projects, the relatively small scale of Loblolly House meant that such proof was not required. Less emphasis was placed upon thermal testing prior to deployment and the building insulation and conditioning systems were designed without including the thermal blanket created in the facade cavity. Nonetheless, this cavity has proven itself effective in reducing heating demand. Loblolly House was subject to a yearlong postinstallation analysis using an array of sensors to monitor exterior temperature and solar radiation, as well as temperatures between the exterior and interior doors. The collected data shows an average buffer of 30 percent between the exterior ambient temperature and the facade cavity temperature. The differential fluctuates with solar radiation: there is less temperature variation on cloudy days and more on sunny days.

The project indicates that with active layers, a double-layer facade can be an effective system for passive conditioning. Unlike a wall with fixed windows, designed for average conditions across a year, this fully adjustable system allows the house to respond to a full range of environmental conditions across all seasons.

In both of these instances of high-performance-facade development, as well as other projects and experiments undertaken by the office, we are guided by our research ethic. Each solution, when monitored and assessed, leads to new questions and suggests further initiatives that can offer improved performance. We are sustained in this process by our ISO quality-control system, which requires not only rigorous planning and action, but also introspective monitoring and learning. Quality control and a strong research ethic form a fully integrated system. Each confronts the other, giving rise to a continuous cycle of innovation and improvement.

NOTES

1. International Organization for Standardization (ISO), "ISO 9001: 2008 Quality management systems— Requirements," ISO, http://www.iso.org/ iso/catalogue_detail?csnumber=21823.

2. Home Delivery: Fabricating the Modern Dwelling exhibition website, "Cellophane House," Museum of Modern Art (MoMA), http://www. momahomedelivery.org.

Material
Ecologies in
Architecture
Blaine Brownell

Architectural Foresight

The world is fundamentally different today than it was yesterday. Our global paradigm is characterized by crumbling energy regimes, dwindling raw materials, fading geopolitical boundaries, global warming, and the radical transformation of our physical environment.

For the first time in human history, more than half the population of the Earth now lives in cities.[1] At the same time, cities are being transformed, often in dysfunctional ways, especially due to endless sprawl. The explosion of urban populations worldwide is now a common topic of concern. Cities are reevaluating smart growth strategies while seeking sophisticated transportation solutions to unprecedented levels of congestion. Meanwhile, energy and material resources continue to be depleted at an accelerated rate, inspiring a host of conservation programs and environmental reforms initiated by both the public and private sectors.

Architecture is currently undergoing one of the most fundamental and unprecedented shifts in its history, both in the eyes of its makers and its users. Given the newfound awareness of humanity's undeniable impact on the health of our planet, coupled with the fact that buildings use roughly half of all resources, a new challenge has arisen that architecture must address.

For as long as we can remember, architects have attended to the fundamental qualities of function and form in their work. Create an edifice that is practical as well as beautiful, we were told, and you have succeeded. However, this simple recipe is no longer sufficient. We know architecture should not merely be a collection of attractive and pragmatic objects that suck large amounts of resources, serve the needs of relatively few people for relatively short periods of time, only to be demolished and injected into the great human waste stream. We now need more from architecture. In addition to function and form, architecture must be imbued with foresight.

Foresight does not simply consider ways to make a building last longer, although durability can be an important component of sustainable thinking. Foresight respects the future health of the environment and the lives of individuals beyond the targeted occupants. Foresight considers the entire ecology of material and energy resources that comprise a work, including their origins and their life after demolition. Foresight contemplates the welfare of the individuals affected by the work, from the building inhabitants to the laborers who manufactured the building materials, perhaps thousands of miles away. Foresight shapes architecture that, like life itself, produces as well as consumes, reincorporates all of its waste, and maintains an ecological footprint in balance with the requirements of its context. Foresight in architecture necessitates a fundamental understanding of the present and future material flows harnessed by building construction and product manufacturing. It is therefore imperative for architects to become more knowledgeable about material resources at both local and global scales. Today, major material shifts are occurring in the domains of energy, resources, and technology, all of which promise profound changes to our physical environment. An understanding of the coming challenges, as well as potential positive solutions to these challenges, will allow architects to lead, rather than follow, the change ahead.

Energy and the Demise of the First Machine Age

We cannot consider the human-made world without regarding the resources used to mine, manufacture, transport, construct, and distribute its physical components. History has shown us the extent to which various civilizations have been shaped by their energy resources, and how complacency in the face of dwindling supplies has led even the greatest empires to collapse.[2]

We may face such a moment today. The international scientific community has suggested we may be nearing the brink of inestimable change, defined by the point at which half the Earth's supply of crude oil has been tapped (peak oil), soon to be followed by the same halfway mark for natural gas. The term *peak* doesn't mean the world will run out of oil; it is simply the point at which accelerating demand meets decelerating supply, a simple law of economics based on limited resources. No one is certain what the outcome will be, but the upheaval of international markets may be the least of our worries.

We are, after all, the great-great-grandchildren of the petroleum era. We may think of ourselves in futuristic terms, and claim to represent the information-age society, yet virtually every aspect of our lives is still defined by the extraction of fuels from fossils.

Our Energy Diet

How did we decide to unleash the energy stored, over billions of years, beneath the Earth's surface as our primary fuel source? It comes as no surprise that humankind will exhaust fossil fuel supplies in a mere blink of the time required to store them. Should we not seek energy sources that may be harnessed "live," in which the rate of depletion never surpasses the rate of storage? Could we not emulate real-time natural models for daily energy use (such as photosynthesis), and save long-stored supplies for peak or emergency uses?

Clearly, the energy use of society has increased exponentially since the dawn of technology. Today, the annual energy diet of the average American is gluttonous indeed; it amounts to the equivalent of 8,000 pounds (3,636 kilograms) of oil, 4,700 pounds (2,136 kilograms) of natural gas, 5,150 pounds (2,340 kilograms) of coal, and one-tenth of a pound (45 grams) of uranium.[3] The United States is home to less than 5 percent of the global population, yet consumes 25 percent of the world's energy.[4] Not surprisingly, rapidly developing nations, such as China and India, desire greater energy shares. But at what cost? Approximately two billion people worldwide lack access to electricity or power.[5] How do we justify such a massive disparity in energy accessibility today?

Energy Regime Change

An answer may reside in the form assumed by our current energy establishment, in which a centralized, hierarchical model, represented by a few large companies, dictates the energy outlook of most of the developed world. Unlike the Internet, which is a massively distributed information network, the fossil fuel regime more closely mimics the form of the early, inefficient, centralized telephone network. Our current energy network has not changed much since the industrial revolution.

American economist Jeremy Rifkin suggests our future energy milieu will closely resemble the Internet in its structure, open access, and lack of centralized control.[6] The nonprofit organization Solar Electric Light Fund, for example, empowers developing communities with stand-alone power-generation systems and safe sources of nighttime illumination, demonstrating that the third world can improve its living standards without dependence on traditional energy networks.[7] In communities with established energy distribution, the combination of high fossil-fuel costs, increased performance in renewable energy technologies, and local incentives, such as rebates and reverse-metering, point to a future comprising self-propagating, semiautonomous networks that share energy over shorter distances than traditional power grids. These networks will be messy and complex, encouraging creative trading partnerships between neighbors seeking to optimize power use while avoiding peak loads. [FIG. 01]

While much of today's alternative energy buzz focuses on "off the grid" strategies, these tendencies are really the desire for freedom from centralized power models. In reality, rather than energy independence in stand-alone situations, we should seek energy interdependence via new models, since power reliability, effectiveness, and use options will likely be superior in a new energy web. The propagation of wireless energy technologies using electromagnetic resonance to convey power over short distances without cables or batteries will facilitate this interdependence.

FIG. 01 School energy-production project, Solar Electric Light Fund, Eastern Cape Province, South Africa, 2008

Like wireless communication networks, wireless power will lead to freedoms and security vulnerabilities, resulting in the development of sophisticated access protocols as well as concerns about the effects of low-level radiation on the body.

Creative Conservation

As energy costs continue to escalate, conservation measures will likewise intensify. In a 2008 exhibition at the Canadian Centre for Architecture examining architecture's response to the 1973 oil crisis, curators Giovanna Borasi and Mirko Zardini remind us of the stark conservation measures mandated by many nations after the OPEC oil embargo, including designated car-free days and imposed curfews on business and nighttime illumination.[8] Given the price of a barrel of oil quadrupled in a little over one year, it comes as no surprise such drastic strategies were implemented.[9]

While the 1970s oil crisis was largely a politically motivated maneuver orchestrated by Arab nations after the peak in United States' oil production, today's crisis relates to the imminent peak in global oil production. In other words, the physical limitations of a natural resource have led to our current situation. While this distinction poses a much larger threat to our current energy status quo, there is hope the change will occur more gradually than during the 1973 oil crisis. More time would mean more creative conservation solutions could be developed.

Some of these solutions will likely come from the study of how nonwestern cultures relate to matters of energy consumption and conservation. The Japanese, for example, believe in conditioning bodies versus space. The focus on heating and cooling people—via high-tech devices, such as infrared-sensing heating, ventilating, and air conditioning (HVAC) systems, or low-tech means, such as increased ventilation in summer, or portable, electric devices in winter—results in considerable savings compared with typical energy use in the United States. This strategy also allows increased natural ventilation, meaning buildings in Japan often have healthier interior environments.

Creative solutions for energy conservation will also include renewed scrutiny of lighting strategies. After all, artificial illumination is used in many circumstances when free daylight exists outside. It is precisely

FIG. 02 Parans Solar Lighting system

because buildings are largely constructed with opaque, light-reducing materials, deep floor plates, and inadequate penetrations, that artificial illumination is so widely required during daylight hours. Artificial lighting not only consumes energy and materials, it adds to the heating load of buildings. However, a new generation of sunlight-delivery systems offers a solution. The Parans Solar Lighting system, manufactured in Sweden, uses fiber-optic technology to deliver sunlight via rooftop magnifying units to remote "skylights" located deep within a structure. [FIG. 02] Tokyo-based Material House's Mirror Duct system functions similarly, reflecting ultraviolet-free light with highly efficient mirrors far inside interior spaces. The delivery of reflected sunlight within building interiors can increase occupant health and outlook, as natural diurnal cycles are reinforced by variations in light levels and coloration. Moreover, interior, daylight-delivery strategies can support plant growth while mitigating mold development in wet areas. These kinds of natural strategies should help architects remember the critical role daylight played in defining space, long before interior conditions could be modified by the flick of a switch.

Growing Materials

Ending our addiction to fossil fuels will also require the development of new alternatives to petroleum-derived products. Bioplastics, for example, will replace traditional plastic with polymers developed from various agricultural products. Corn-derived polylactic acid (PLA) has already replaced a significant percentage of petroleum-based plastic packaging in the consumer market, and wood fibers from rapidly renewable plants like kenaf may be incorporated with PLA to produce sturdier, longer-lasting products such as cell phone shells, laptop casings, and automobile body parts. [FIG. 03] Many bioplastics also possess properties superior to traditional plastics, such as biodegradability, shape-memory capabilities, and 100 percent horizontal recyclability. Like biofuels, however, bioplastics production raises the ethical dilemma of appropriating food substances for other uses. Using agricultural products to provide energy or create new consumer goods rather than feed people will likely be one of the great controversies of the current century.

Reducing energy embodied in materials will also be an important strategy for mitigating our petroleum dependency. Since the discovery of fire, humankind has used heat extensively in the manufacture of materials. Despite the fact material production methods have become increasingly sophisticated over time, we still use the "heat, beat, and treat" method of manufacture, employing great amounts of heat, pressure, and processing to synthesize stuff from natural resources. The result is that our constructed environment is largely "cooked." Constructed from concrete, wood, steel, brick, glass, and so on, the buildings and cities that

FIG. 03 Vehicle built with kenaf-reinforced plastic, Toyota, i-Unit concept vehicle, 2005

surround us retain the record of the vast quantities of expended energy required for their existence. However, there is an alternative model that promises to reduce or eliminate this embodied energy, as well as redefine conventional manufacturing methodologies. Biomimicry, or biomimetic design, looks to natural principles for inspiration and guidance.[10] In terms of fabrication, nature creates many materials—some of them many times stronger than our best performers—using biochemical methods. Mimicking these processes means growing materials rather than manufacturing them.

Rethinking Resources

I once saw a bumper sticker that read "If you ever had enough, would you know it?" This simple phrase delivers a sobering blow to our consumption-based zeitgeist. Although it is uncomfortable to contemplate, we need to consider: Would most of us, given the chance, live up to whatever living standard we were afforded, no matter how luxurious or prodigal in nature? Don't we all seek more than we currently have? But how many bedrooms do we really need? How many cars, computers, or calories, for that matter?

The point here is not to instill guilt, but to encourage awareness about what resources fulfilling lives truly require. Until recently, there have been few means for determining an individual resource-allocation standard, so it is no wonder, in a throw away economy, we have rarely considered such a notion. However, researchers are developing an increasingly accurate picture of our ecological footprint.

Scientists now tell us that we exceeded the world's ability to sustain our current lifestyle during the late 1980s, at which point we began using natural resources faster than the rate of replenishment. According to the World Wide Fund for Nature's 2004 *Living Planet Report*, society's ecological footprint outstripped the globe's capacity by twenty percent in 2001.[11]

Citing a recent United States Geological Society study, American environmentalist Lester Brown informs us that we will exhaust known stores of several metals, including lead, copper, iron ore, and aluminum, vital to construction and other industries, within the next two to three generations.[12] Although recycling efforts have accelerated, virgin materials are still being harvested at an alarming rate. Metals aren't the only substances being rapidly depleted; timber extraction is also highly controversial, with the near disappearance of old-growth forests worldwide via uncontrolled land development and deforestation.

What will the world be like when virgin materials become too expensive, difficult, or controversial to harvest or extract? The average building today relies upon a great quantity of these resources for its construction. Faced with these facts, we can easily imagine a future in which industry has completely reengineered its handling of material resources. After all, there seems to be no other choice.

Coming to Terms with Waste

As if resource extraction isn't bad enough, we must also consider its evil twin: waste. *Homo sapiens* is the only species that creates what may be truly considered waste (matter that is difficult to reincorporate into the natural cycle). We create waste coming and going, creating and destroying, preserving and dismantling. The construction industry is the most wasteful, with 136 million tons of construction debris generated annually in the United States.[13]

Not the least of our concerns is the waste produced in the form of greenhouse gases resulting from industrial processes and construction activities. The embodied energy present within new products and materials also indicates proportional amounts of carbon dioxide released into the atmosphere during their manufacture. Concrete is responsible for 7 to 10 percent of global carbon dioxide emissions, making it the third largest contributor to global warming after transportation and power-generation.[14]

Dematerialization

Predictably, the relative resource consumption levels of materials are being carefully examined, resulting in less-substantial products that perform similar to or better than their predecessors. From the Stone Age to today's era of advanced fibers, there has been an accelerated thinning of materials. The recently developed synthetic fiber Zylon, for example, possesses approximately twice the tensile strength of steel and twice the tensile modulus of Kevlar, not to mention unprecedented lightness and fire resistance.[15] Common materials like concrete are also being transformed via lower-embodied-energy cements and lightweight high-performance aggregates, generating products with half the weight, better thermal resistance, and similar strength to conventional concrete.[16]

One of the results of this trend is that, in general, architectural cladding has become thinner and more complex over time. If we were to graph the thickness of the wall over time, we would witness the emergence of an accelerated trend line, from the stone walls of Egyptian temples to modern curtain wall structures. The wall cavity has also become more intricate, with multiple layers of materials designed to perform a variety of functions, including solar radiation mitigation, moisture protection, and insulation.

Another intriguing development concerns dematerialization, in the form of increased light- and view-transmittance in architecture. Optical-fiber-embedded, light-transmitting concrete, for example, conveys significant levels of illumination and crisp shadows through a medium historically associated with solidity and opacity. [FIG. 04] High-alumina and corundum ceramics likewise yield strikingly transparent materials with high strength, hardness, and wear resistance. Aerogel-infused building panels make light transmittance possible within insulated, fire-resistant cladding systems. These technologies indicate a compelling, potential future for architectural illumination and point to the dissolution of a clear boundary between the wall and the window in architecture. As light- and image-conveying materials become endowed with "wall-like" properties related to structure, thermal performance, and fire resistance, we will continue to witness the deopacification of the wall.

Renewal

Materials are also being studied for their potential to lead second lives, rather than be disposed of as waste once they have served their originally intended purpose. The escalating buzz surrounding the environmental movement, accompanied by trends like the self-described Lifestyles of Health and Sustainability (LOHAS) market segment, highlights a newly emerging, aesthetic predisposition. Personal products and accessories made with reused content increasingly garner positive status due to the more meaningful message carried by "recycled chic" versus the generic consumerism of luxury brand-names.

FIG. 04 Litracon Light Transmitting Concrete, Bachmann Architects, Museum
Cella Septichora, Pecs, Hungary, 2006

This movement informs us that trash can be transformed into art,
a fact that alters the problem from how many resources do we need, to
how creatively can we use the resources we have? When the least wanted
materials are incorporated into the most desirable products, we realize the power of design. However, the waste challenge is significant
enough to merit not only product-level solutions, but also applications
at architectural and infrastructural scales. Manufacturers have begun to
fabricate building surfaces containing high percentages of repurposed
waste, such as solid-surface countertops made completely of household,
high-density polyethelene (HDPE) containers, and translucent wall panels
made of fused waste glass from building construction sites. Alternative
architectural practices—exemplified by operations such as Rural Studio,
ZEDFactory, and the Office of Mobile Design—likewise demonstrate that
design can be just as much a creative form of reconnaissance as synthesis,
because the act of seeking out salvage materials for reuse in construction
can often yield promising and highly unexpected design results, while
using fewer virgin resources and diverting existing material from the
waste-stream. In this way, an architecture generated through salvage may
impart deeper meaning than one comprising virgin resources.

Another important factor related to waste is the production of material byproducts, such as volatile organic compounds (VOCs) that degrade
environmental quality. While much attention has been paid recently to
reducing the VOC levels in materials such as carpet, paint, and sealants,

another trend promises to upend conventional strategies for improving air quality. Using the photocatalyzing properties exhibited by compounds like titanium dioxide, new cements, such as used in Italcementi's TX Active concrete, and paints, such as Reben, have been formulated to reduce ambient air pollution in the presence of sunlight. Rather than simply degrading environmental conditions less than their conventional peers, these products improve them. [FIG. 05] Considering the unprecedented levels of pervasive pollutants now present throughout the globe, this trend promises to play a much-needed role in remediating the environment.

The Living Machine

When Silicon Valley pundit Kevin Kelly talks about technology, he personifies it as a global-scale entity with its own desires and predispositions. Technology wants to increase its own ubiquity, power, accessibility, and replicability, he claims.[17] When we look at trends in technology—charting computational power against time, for example—a parabolic arc emerges indicating the consistent acceleration of technological development. After four decades, we are witnessing the perpetuation of Intel cofounder Gordon Moore's observation that computational density doubles within a given unit of time. However, what happens when change occurs too fast? What will it be like when the gentle curve approaches a vertical line— when Moore's Law becomes Moore's Wall? For example, how will we

FIG. 05 Italcementi's TX Active concrete, Richard Meier & Partners, Jubilee Church, Rome, Italy, 1996–2003

respond to technologies that advance every second at a rate that used to require a month? Environmentalist Stewart Brand, inventor Ray Kurzweil, and others describe this moment, called a singularity, as a point at which the old rules change and we enter a new epoch defined by a completely new set of circumstances.[18]

It is clear a significant transformation is taking place within the fields of design and architecture resulting from the dramatic influx of new materials and technologies. Influential thinkers in fields as diverse as biomedicine (Francis Crick), philosophy (Manuel De Landa), and economics (John Young) point to a new materialism brought about by advances in science and an increasing awareness of humankind's physical influence on the Earth.

In the spirit of Kevin Kelly, author of *Out of Control*, one could imagine technology has become aware of its effect on the planet and is adapting accordingly.[19] Traditional models of technology position it in contrast to nature, but as technology becomes increasingly sophisticated the lines begin to blur. The nanoscale experiments occurring in laboratories, the endeavor to map and manipulate life's genetic code, the development of parallel computing and complex networks, and emerging biomimetic technologies and manufacturing processes, all point to the gradual merging of the mechanical with the biological. If technology is, in fact, now becoming conscious of resource limitations, perhaps it will work more in concert with nature than against it. For example, cleanup efforts are being conducted in China's rivers, Kelly states, not only for health reasons, but also because silicon chip manufacturers require clean water.[20] Closed-loop manufacturing processes, which operate more like natural models than industrial-era methods, have been shown to make efficient use of materials, significantly reduce or eliminate waste, and create economic success.

Smart Technologies

One of the most environmentally friendly developments in building technology is the capability to monitor and regulate energy and resource consumption. Since the beginning of the industrial revolution, widespread consumption of cheap energy from fossil-fuel sources has promoted waste; today, however, rising energy costs encourage conservation measures, and building-integrated, resource-monitoring technologies can prove economically viable over time. For example, Stephen Gage and Will Thorne have proposed a collection of facade-roving robots, called "edge monkeys," that monitor energy use by checking windows, regulating blinds, monitoring thermostats, and even signaling building occupants regarding their own energy consumption. [FIGS. 06-09] Less technologically sophisticated approaches include building-integrated daylighting systems with photo sensors, automated operable louvers, and dimmable lighting controls. These technologies make design a spatiotemporal affair: interactive systems like these have the ability to influence form directly, and are therefore like architectural editors, continually tweaking and adjusting the performance—and aesthetics—of architecture.

This persistent transformational quality is, after all, more like life itself, and the architect's role shifts from that of a musician playing a fixed performance to that of a director orchestrating a collection of diverse, semiautonomous players. As today's material revolutionaries coax technology toward a more diverse, complex, and specialized future, we are witnessing the mechanical age shift into the biomimetic age. Although current examples emulate living systems in terms of form or performance, future materials will also emulate life in their fabrication, and products will be grown rather than manufactured.

Material Frontiers and the Architect

During previous material epochs, humankind privileged the development of particular materials over others, such as the focus on metallurgy in the mid-twentieth century. We now live in a time in which all material frontiers are being explored at once. Materials science advances are unprecedented in their number, diversity, and distribution. With regard to construction materials, we only have to pick up a recent design industry journal to see the extent to which manufacturers are scrutinizing and retooling their product lines. Increased awareness concerning changes in energy, resource allocation, and technology has led to a veritable explosion of creative material solutions, and these solutions are increasingly taking cues from natural systems. The establishment of distributed, semiautonomous, renewable-energy communities; the trajectory toward closed-loop fabrication and the creative transformation of waste into

Time = 0

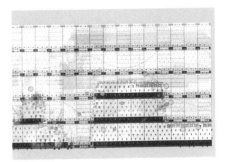

FIGS. 06-07 Edge Monkey
behavior diagrams, Stephen
Gage and Will Thorne, Edge
Monkeys, 2005

time + 1.5

time + 3

FIG. 08 Edge Monkey
mechanism, Stephen Gage
and Will Thorne, Edge
Monkeys, 2005

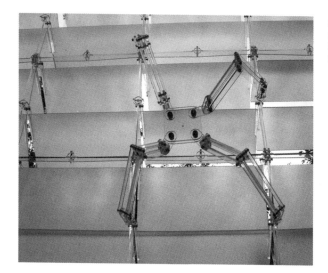

FIG. 09 Edge Monkey in its habitat, Stephen Gage and Will Thorne, Edge Monkeys, 2005

art; as well as the increased sophistication, diversity, and interactivity of technology, all highlight a positive trend toward biomimesis, albeit at an early stage.

In this brave new world for architecture, architects must place as much emphasis on research and teaching as they do on practice, because the complexities of future challenges and the expertise required for new solutions leave us no other choice. Tomorrow's architect will possess a thorough grounding in materials science, the mechanics of industrial ecology, and advanced environmental building practices. She will be a vigilant student of technology and its future directions, incorporating innovative techniques, products, and systems as appropriate, in order to push the boundaries of architecture. Moreover, the future architect will also be actively engaged in the public realm, creating profound connections with leaders in other fields and advocating the power of design through far-reaching, collaborative endeavors. In this way, tomorrow's architect may act as a catalyst, releasing the creative potential inherent within all people for the betterment of the physical environment.

Let us not forget change is imminent. Clearly, serious consideration of issues relating to material flows and processes in architecture will be essential. There has never been a better time for architecture to live up to its full potential and demonstrate its value to all. The future is here, and every one of us has a stake in it.

NOTES

1. NC State University news, "Mayday
23: World Population Becomes More
Urban Than Rural," North Carolina State
University, May 22, 2007, http://news.ncsu.
edu/releases/2007/may/104.html.

2. Joseph A. Tainter, *The Collapse of
Complex Societies* (Cambridge: Cambridge
University Press, 1990).

3. Walter Youngquist, *GeoDestinies:
The Inevitable Control of Earth Resources
over Nations and Individuals* (Portland, OR:
National Book Company, 1997), 22.

4. World Resources Institute, National
Environment Programme, United Nations
Development Programme, and the World
Bank, *World Resources 1996–97: A Guide
to the Global Environment* (Oxford: Oxford
University Press, 1996).

5. The World Bank, *Rural Energy and
Development: Improving Energy Supplies
for Two Billion People* (Washington, DC:
World Bank, 1996).

6. Jeremy Rifkin, *The Hydrogen
Economy: The Creation of the Worldwide
Energy Web and the Redistribution of Power
on Earth* (New York: J. P. Tarcher, 2003).

7. Solar Electric Light Fund, http://
www.self.org.

8. Giovanna Borasi and Mirko Zardini,
eds., *Sorry, Out of Gas: Architecture's
Response to the 1973 Oil Crisis* (Montreal:
Canadian Centre for Architecture, 2007),
54–55.

9. Ibid.

10. Janine M. Benyus, *Biomimicry:
Innovation Inspired by Nature* (New York:
Perennial, 2002).

11. World Wide Fund for Nature,
et al., *Living Planet Report 2004* (Gland,
Switzerland: World Wide Fund for Nature,
2004), 1.

12. Lester Brown, *Plan B 2.0: Rescuing
a Planet Under Stress and a Civilization in
Trouble* (New York: W. W. Norton, 2006),
109.

13. Ken Sandler, "Analyzing What's
Recyclable in C&D Debris," *BioCycle*
(November, 2003): 52.f.

14. Jeremy Faludi, "Concrete: A
'Burning' Issue," World Changing,
http://www.worldchanging.com/
archives/001610.html.

15. Toyobo Co., http://www.toyobo.
co.jp/e/index.htm.

16. HySSIL, http://www.hyssil.com.

17. Kevin Kelly, "What Does
Technology Want?" Lecture at the
Pop!Tech conference, Camden, Maine,
October 19, 2006.

18. Stewart Brand, *The Clock of the
Long Now: Time and Responsibility* (New
York: Basic Books, 2000), 17.

19. Kevin Kelly, *Out of Control: The
New Biology of Machines, Social Systems,
and the Economic World* (Reading, MA:
Addison-Wesley, 1994).

20. Kelly, "What Does Technology
Want?"

Toward a Productive Excess

Beth Blostein

India's ancient Sun Temple at Konark was uncovered in the nineteenth century, engulfed in a forest and shrouded from view. The Sun Temple is a riddle of multivalent symbolism, celebrating the Hindu sun god, Sūrya, and the life-sustaining power he embodied. Mortarless, precision-fitting carved stonework, once said to be held together by strong magnetic forces generated by the material's assemblage, depicted Sūrya as a seven-horse chariot driving energy across the sky. The Temple was an architectural mechanism to transform light energy into a dynamically tactile and culturally meaningful visual event. This operative and essential relationship between energy and architecture, and, in particular, a controlled negotiation of light and surface, persists today.[1]

One might describe this relationship between the temple and the sun as bionomic—there is a connection between material artifacts, energy's affects, and the biological, psychological, or spiritual condition of an ecology. The vitality of any ecology is directly bound to its ability to answer the call to action, to effectively and productively use available energy, so that it can continue to operate on and within its physical domain. All living things are held to this contract.

Today, far from the days when sun worship was a central component of global order, energy—the primordial ooze of ecologies, its use and misuse, conservation and depletion, is one of the most contentious issues on the global scene. Of course, energy—now in its nonrenewable forms (for example, oil, natural gas)—is still closely associated with political power and control. But more generally, what else can be said about energy? How can we begin to unravel its complexities? David Nye says:

> "Energy" may be a noun, but it refers to neither a solid thing like a shoe nor to an abstraction like "liberty" or "democracy." It might be said that this noun aspires to be a verb, since it refers to an active,

almost simultaneous, movement from one state to another. Energy is both a commodity and fundamental aspect of being.[2]

Given this unusual status, Nye argues that energy has become a "prize to be won."[3]

In the late 1800s and early 1900s energy was uncoupled from the shackles of human labor by new technologies for power generation and transmission; its ubiquity was driven by dams, power lines, and utility companies. The agility of electricity allowed energy to effortlessly navigate the landscape and perpetuate development no longer reliant on adjacencies between energy sources and productive operations. Its omnipresence set the stage for the shameless exploitation of its potential; the pernicious claim to the energy prize was much like hanging a deer head above the mantle. This is particularly evident in cities such as Los Angeles and Phoenix, which have grown exponentially despite the fact that they rely on the transmission of electricity from distant locales.

A pivotal moment in this euphoric exploitation was the Panama-Pacific International Exposition of 1915 held in San Francisco. Before this time, the cost of electrical energy and artificial lighting was high and considered a luxury item beyond the reach of the average person. With the focal point of the exposition, the Tower of Jewels, consumption transgressed beyond the satisfaction of basic needs into the realm of spectacular effect. The 435-foot-high structure was encrusted with 100,000 hand-cut crystals, specifically placed to refract and reflect light supplied by the new technology of floodlighting, a high-powered incarnation of the humble lighting that provided for basic needs.[4] The tower's surfaces, absorbing energy into a surreal and fiery image, became couture. [FIG. 01] The result was an exuberant show of special effects, elevating the creation of artificial light to divine status; a prophetically irreverent alliance between desire and consumption was born, and architecture was a culpable player.

Fast-forward to the 1960s. Reactionary environmental responsiveness was becoming a prominent theme within various art and design circles. In the cultural arena, artists like Robert Smithson embraced the topic by engaging directly with polluted or compromised sites. And, notably, the foresightful architect Buckminster Fuller was concerned with the limits of natural resources available on "Spaceship Earth," proffering designs

FIG. 01 Tower of Jewels, Thomas Hastings, San Francisco Panama-Pacific International Exposition, 1915

intended to make a minimal impact on the planet.[5] Soon to follow, in the 1970s political arena, Jimmy Carter was a leading figure recognizing the wanton wastefulness of energy as a global problem. Trained as an engineer, hoping for a career on a nuclear submarine, Carter understood the problem of entropy: that energy, over time, would become less available. His deployment of a national energy policy was a reflection of that understanding.

The first decade of the twenty-first century presented the world with a primary crisis of contemporary life: our global consumption trends allowed us to ignore, or sidestep, the specter of entropic decline. The forecasts in the '60s and '70s of the irreversible and progressive dispersal of our world's energy and matter into a homogeneous amalgamation gained new momentum, even as efforts to minimize or reverse the dispersal gained prominence. What happened?

The form of energy the majority of humanity has come to rely upon does not come to us naturally or easily, but it does seem to flow rather freely within the developed world and to others with capital. Part of a highly complex infrastructure, energy of all forms is generated behind the scenes. To arrive at our pumps, stoves, and switches, resources must be drilled, compressed, burned, refined, bought, sold, and traded. This increasingly painful process of coaxing useful energy from our finite supply of fossil fuels comes with a price, and the bill is sealed and delivered with easily ignored, yet all-too-familiar, consequences, such as global warming, pollution, and exponential monetary inflation.

Aside from the environmental perils associated with its capture and manipulation, energy produces stuff. Those with an abundance of energy—meaning those who have the economic and political means to gain access—use the resource to collect more stuff. This production and collection of exponential amounts of stuff allows energy to become visible, through valuable innovation and the production of the ever-higher-tech (and soon to be obsolete) consumables. Unfortunately, within these new consumables are high levels of irretrievable, embodied energy and complex waste. Together these "stuff by-products" form indissoluble agglomerations that wander the planet looking for a resting place. One striking example is a massive trash heap, twice the size of Texas, which floats somewhere between San Francisco and Hawaii. The 3.5-million-ton "Great Pacific Garbage Patch" is 80 percent plastic. Like the legendary ghost ship, the Flying Dutchman, doomed to sail the oceans without relief from land, the Great Patch has been trapped in a circular course by winds and currents since its birth in the 1950s. Its circumference grows tenfold every decade as it accumulates the latest fashions in trash that have made their way into the Pacific.[6] So while it is true that energy is becoming less available (the promise of entropy), modern matter and its undesirable by-products proliferate and accumulate.

This rambling excess of expelled matter might be considered a contemporary, perverse, example of Georges Bataille's accursed share. Published in 1949, ironically about the same time the Great Patch was spawned, Bataille argued a mandate to give, or surrender, a portion of one's lot came with the achievement of economic wealth in developed societies. This "excess," he argued, is destined either for productive use, in the arts or economic investment, or for spectacular and luxurious expenditures, such as monuments and wars. This is the "accursed share"; a society must determine how and in what form its excess will be distributed.[7] It could take the form of food, or humanitarian or monetary aid. On the surface, such transfers appear highly altruistic, but they can sometimes serve to exacerbate the differences between a world of the "haves" and the "have-nots." On the one hand there are those with an abundance of energy and resources (those with the biggest or the most), and on the other there are those unable to afford or access the prize (those who cannot even muster the smallest). The have-nots become the ones who unwittingly accept the "gifts" (sometimes trash heaps) of others.

This accepted vision of energy as something resembling an unstable commodity—something that can be drawn into the fold of personal, political, and societal conquest—orders our outlook for a sustainable future today. Popular culture imagines an energy endgame in dystopic films like *Mad Max 2*, where we are left to wander the planet in our supercharged 1973 Ford Falcons fighting for the remaining energy.[8] This vision is insufficient; it destroys energy's aspiration to be a continually active and productive agent in the world. Less abundant energy is fought over, hoarded, and refigured into lifeless by-products.

We might argue that current strategies to sustain our planet may, in fact, subscribe to this insufficient vision. One strategic reaction is to *shuffle*. A mechanism for shuffling is the "carbon credit," intended to put a cap on global annual greenhouse-gas emissions. Like monetary stock, these credits are subject to fluctuating international market demands. An especially green performance (high productivity plus high environmental responsibility) by one company leads to a surplus of credits available for acquisition by another company. Another mechanism for shuffling is the artificial "carbon sink," where networks of operation are extended to include interest in super "eco" projects. These projects, constructed land and forest reservoirs, counter their disconnected, mirrored reality by storing carbon emissions transferred from the locations that produced them. These artificial mechanisms create an illusion of equilibrium within what is, in fact, a highly reordered and distorted ecology. Based on the assumption that a problem in one place can be solved somewhere else by theoretically balancing the scales that measure overall energy consumption and environmental health, they offer a false reality. While the construction of this "inverted doppelgänger" is beneficial for some, it produces unnatural friction in its environmental shadows and on its edges. Those living within the borders of an offending geography are overly susceptible to environmental hazards, while the "sink" provides an oasis of hypercleanliness for others.

Another popular strategic reaction to instability is to *reduce*. This intuitive (and politically correct) reaction resists current energy regimes by trying to make consumption more efficient; it tries to minimize, or even stop, the flow of energy born from finite resources. Again the built world of architecture and its relationship to the elusive forces of energy are brought to bear, responsible for up to 40 percent of the total annual global energy consumption.[9] The surfaces, products, and techniques of architecture persist as a primary site of engagement with the energy problem. From hyperinsulating skins and the "Energy Star" appliances they contain, to the occupant-sensing thermostats and shading devices that automate dynamic responsiveness—these are all accepted technological sentinels of the reduction strategy.

Doubtless both green crediting and energy reduction are nontrivial and much-needed strategies that give architecture the opportunity to offset the delightfully excessive Tower of Jewels. But given our current course, it is very difficult to imagine a world where we forever sustain concern for every flip of the light switch and the greenhouse gas emissions that each of our actions entails. Added to this, more countries are successfully striving to raise their standard of living—namely China and India—with potentially dramatic consequences for global energy use. Moreover, in a global economy—and despite our smaller, smarter packages—our heaps, patches, and fills increasingly travel the planet to be received by unwitting recipients. Richard Duncan, director of the Institute on Energy and Man, asserts the Stone Age represented a sustainable way of life insofar as there was a humble relationship between humanity's use of natural resources and their supply. He suggests we might be forced to consider this age a model of how we should live today.[10] Is a world sans the multitude of mobile devices that now surround us something we can really fathom, let alone stomach? Is minimizing the flow of energy or a green-credited fabrication of a remote-yet-balanced ecology the complete answer? These strategies suggest a world without excess in any form.

Emerging techniques and practices are increasingly working to recalibrate the situation in a new way, developing unique design ecologies and providing a productive addition to the twin reactions of *shuffling* and *reducing*. Architecture is a poster child for such efforts; its articulated surfaces are now donned in energy-producing, green couture. KieranTimberlake's SmartWrap is a prime example of the proliferation of materials that leave behind the disconnected-energy generation, exemplified by the miles of power lines that articulate the urban to rural fields, to become a new form of energy ornament, compressed onto architecture. While the 1990s saw media screens and information as a contemporary manifestation of architectural ornament, "green" will play the part in this era. More than an accessory or trope for an information-saturated culture, however, this ornament is productive, transforming nutrients supplied by nature into food for architecture and its inhabitants. The surface, the ongoing preoccupation of much architectural experimentation, and its program as canvas and boundary, is now further problematized by its new obligation as energy generator: engaging, absorbing, and transfiguring nature into useful elements.

There are precedents for perhaps an even more powerful position for this productive entwinement of architecture and energy, and a different agenda for their interface. In the early years of the twentieth century, architects, such as the German expressionist Eric Mendelsohn, the French art deco designer Henri Sauvage, and the American Beaux-Arts practitioners Charles Reed and Allen Stem, designed power stations as stylish civic monuments. Within the city, architecture and energy generation—each being absolutely distinguished by the division between energy making on the inside and architectural iconography on the outside— were one. However, as concern for the hygienic conditions within cities escalated and the effects of energy production's filth-spewing processes became intolerable, the site of energy production was removed from its architectural skin and exiled to the urban periphery; energy lost its place as a simultaneously productive cultural and urban endeavor.

Italian architect Antonio Sant'Elia, in his La Città Nuova drawings of 1913–14, suggested a more radical vision for the role of architecture and energy generation when he placed the power station at the center of Milan of the future. The great architectural dynamo literally and figuratively exuded life-giving energy.[11] Unlike the examples of Mendelsohn, Sauvage, Reed, and Stem, Sant'Elia externalized the machinations of power

FIG. 02 Electric Power Plant, Antonio Sant'Elia, La Città Nuova, 1914

generation as the central component of a network, or collective, operating at the urban scale. [FIG. 02] While the Tower of Jewels was a singular condition being constructed under the auspices of the spectacular, Sant'Elia envisioned a spectacular infrastructure.

Following the urban infrastructural model of Sant'Elia, contemporary architecture, with its new, energy-generating green couture, has an opportunity to invest in the making of a new kind of city. To do so, we must *embrace* and *amplify*, rather than merely *shuffle* or *reduce*, the flow of energy. This notion must operate at multiple scales: from local ecologies, such as a single building and its zone of influence, to increasingly complex fields that network architecture, landscapes, and people, ultimately transgressing extant geographic and cultural boundaries. What might emerge is a model of energy as an ever-convertible, fluid asset, one not contained, "credited," or coveted by any particular set of dependencies or medium.

We have already identified successful architectural new beginnings (the high-tech building envelopes, the energy-efficient appliances, the automatic sensing devices) that have impact at the scale of local ecologies.

FIG. 03 City of Light, diorama of Manhattan, Walter Dorwin Teague, World's Fair, New York, 1939
© Bettman/CORBIS

To expand these fields requires an intensification of effort; nothing short of a renewed architectural exuberance is required. Less than twenty-five years after the 1915 Panama-Pacific International Exposition, the City of Light (1939) resurrected a discussion of the Tower of Jewels. The City of Light was the world's largest diorama, built by Con Edison for the World's Fair in Flushing Meadows, New York; it was intended to illustrate how the city and electrical energy would collaborate to support the future of the world.[12] Instead of projecting an image of pure consumption (an architecture of irrational exuberance), the City of Light exuded the excess productivity that was the promise of a twenty-four-hour city—a more rational exuberance. [FIG. 03] In contemporary work, such as the reptilian scene of Studio Formwork's Solar Skins, we can again glimpse the possibility of a productive, articulated, urban-energy field—where the whole exceeds the sum of its parts—as projected in the City of Light's field of glowing apertures. [FIGS. 04-05] Through this collective, hivelike mentality, we move beyond the spectacle of the single, introverted building into the continuous, network ecology of the city that teems with productive activity. The actions of the individual contribute to a collective agenda.

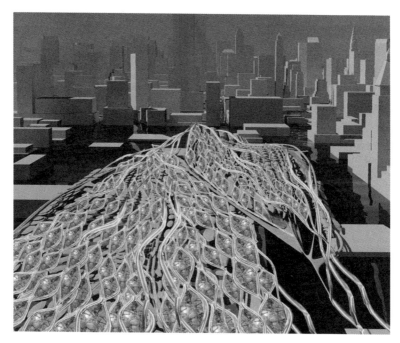

FIGS. 04-05 Solar Skin, Studio Formwork, 2008

FIGS. 06-07 2012 Olympic Stadium, HOK, London, England

This emerging network ecology connects to expansive networks. Consider HOK's stadium for the 2012 London Olympics, designed to be disassembled after the games, shipped across the Atlantic, and rebuilt for the next Olympic hopeful, Chicago.[13] This scenario has obvious energy and material efficiencies. More interesting is the fact that this model could put less-advantaged countries—ones that cannot afford the necessary construction—in a position to play host. These transferable gifts hold the potential to activate a series of environmental and cultural events. [FIGS. 06-07]

Out of necessity, a new relationship between nature and the constructed world is emerging, and energy, in all of its manifestations and extensions, will be the material that negotiates and adorns. Unlike the Great Patch, the by-products of this relationship are obsessively pure, excessively useful. These highly processed resources have no precedent, even in the ideal landscapes portrayed by the likes of French painters Claude Lorraine or Nicolas Poussin, where the powerful environment existed in uncanny harmony with a sublimated constructed world. As a large-scale endeavor, this exuberant, pervasive energy production will allow contemporary culture and its technological needs to thrive and develop, and allow a place again for the delight of excess. Works by media artists like the Australian company the Electric Canvas merge architecture and digital media into one new being, the transformation so complete it is difficult to disassemble. With an exuberance not unlike the Tower of Jewels, the artists in the Electric Canvas used projected light and image to seamlessly dress the National Museum of Singapore as a high-tech, smart spectacle that drew hoards of people to the Night Festival. [FIG. 08] But projects such as this have little room in an ecology organized around *shuffling* or *reducing*, where all decisions are driven by the need to control and curtail. Perhaps we have a cultural need or sweet tooth for this form of excess.

During an archaeological dig in Egypt in 1954, a "solar barge" was uncovered at the Giza pyramid complex. This vessel, upon which the sun was believed to arrive and depart, appears in a multitude of permutations throughout the ancient world—it was a world, after all, where a solitary god with a singular embodiment was insufficient.[14] Our cultural delight in the excessive might resurrect this image as a contemporary manifestation.

FIG. 08 Light Festival, the Electric Canvas, National Museum of Singapore, 2008

Our global needs, wants, and crises require our designed world, its land-scapes, and buildings, to come together as a flotilla, to exude the passion of a mob, to contribute to this new form of productive excess.

NOTES

1. Alice Boner, *New light on the Sun Temple of Konārka*, trans. Alice Boner and Sadāśiva Rath Śarmā (Varanasi: Chowkhamba Sanskrit Series Office, 1972).

2. David Nye, *Narratives and Spaces: Technology and the Construction of American Culture* (New York: Columbia University Press, 1997), 75.

3. Ibid.

4. Ibid., 42.

5. Buckminster Fuller, *Buckminster Fuller: Anthology for The New Millennium*, ed. Thomas T. K. Zung (New York: St. Martin's, 2002).

6. The Institute for Figuring, "The Great Pacific Garbage Patch," http://www.theiff.org/reef/reef4.html.

7. Georges Bataille, *The Accursed Share: An Essay on General Economy, Volume 1: Consumption*, trans. Robert Hurley (New York: Zone Books, 1991).

8. Adrian Martin, *The Mad Max Movies* (Sydney and Canberra: Currency Press and Screenbound, 2003).

9. United Nations Environment Program, "Buildings Can Play a Key Role in Combating Climate Change," March 29, 2007, http://www.unep.org/Documents.Multilingual/Default.asp?DocumentID=50 2&ArticleID=5545&l=en.

10. Richard Duncan, "The Peak of World Oil Production and the Road to the Olduvai Gorge," (paper presented at the Pardee Keynote Symposium, Summit 2000, Geological Society of America, Reno, NV, November 13, 2000).

11. Esther da Costa Meyer, *The Work of Antonio Sant'Elia* (New Haven: Yale University Press, 1995), 108–110.

12. Helen A. Harrison, *Dawn of a New Day: The New York World's Fair, 1939/40* (New York: Queens Museum, 1980).

13. Robert Booth, "For Sale: Flatpack Stadium Suitable for Olympic Games," *Guardian*, May 27, 2008, http://www.guardian.co.uk/uk/2008/may/27/olympics2012.london.

14. W. M. Flinders Petrie, *Pyramids and Temples of Gizeh* (New York: Kegan Paul, 2003).

Image Credits

Design and the Welfare of All Life
Figs. 1–5: Courtesy Bruce Mau
Design, Inc.

Weeding the City of Unsustainable Cooling, or, Many Designs rather than Massive Design
Figs. 1–3: Photos by Alexander Porter.

Ecologies of Access
Fig. 1: Courtesy Jim Turner.
Fig. 2: Courtesy of *COLORS MAGAZINE / Colors 71*. Fig. 3: Courtesy Stewart Brand/Jim Turner. Fig. 4: Secondary Cover by Christopher Springman From *Rolling Stone*, July 8, 1971. © Rolling Stone LLC 1971. All Rights Reserved. Reprinted by Permission. Fig. 5: Courtesy Stewart Brand/Jim Turner. Fig. 8 (left): Courtesy Stewart Brand/Jim Turner. Fig. 8 (right): Courtesy Barrett Lyon, The Opte Project. Fig. 9: Courtesy Bruce Mau Design, Inc.

APE
Fig. 2: Courtesy Library of Congress. Fig. 5: Courtesy Atelier Ten. Fig. 6: Courtesy R&Sie(n).

I'mlostinParis
Figs. 1–5: Courtesy R&Sie(n).

Green Screens: Modernism's Secret Garden
Figs. 1–3: © Kazys Varnelis / AUDC

Pneuma: An Indeterminate Architecture, or, Toward a Soft and Weedy Architecture
Figs. 1–3: Courtesy Peter Hasdell.
Fig. 4: Reproduced from Ernest Haeckel, *Kunstformen der Natur*, 1899, plate 84. Fig. 5: Reproduced from D'Arcy Wentworth Thompson, *On Growth and Form*, 1917, figure 166. Figs. 6–9: Courtesy Peter Hasdell.

Tabling Ecologies and Furnishing Performance
Figs. 1–2: Images from Wikipedia Commons, Wikimedia Foundation, Inc. Figs. 3–8: © Stephen Turk

Public Farm 1 (P.F.1)
Figs. 3–6: Photos by Elizabeth Felicella. Figs. 7–8: Courtesy WORKac. Fig. 9: Courtesy Konrad Fiedler. Figs. 10–11: Photos by Elizabeth Felicella.

Float On: A Succession of Progressive Architectural Ecologies
Figs. 1–2: Source: György Kepes, ed., *Arts of the Environment* (Henley, UK: Aidan Ellis, 1972), 192–93. Permission courtesy Juan Navarro Baldeweg. Figs. 3–4: Courtesy MVRDV. Fig. 5: Courtesy Rob 't Hart.

Big Nature
Fig. 1: Courtesy PEG Office of Landscape + Architecture.
Fig. 2: Courtesy Inside Outside.
Fig. 3: Photo by Jitze Couperus.
Figs. 4–5: Courtesy Ashley Kelly and Rikako Wakabayashi, Urban Found Architecture. Fig. 6: Courtesy Philippe Coignet, Office of Landscape Morphology.
Fig. 7: Courtesy Gross.Max.
Fig. 8: Courtesy SLA Architects.

Garden for a Plant Collector, Glasgow
Figs. 1–4: Courtesy Gross.Max.

Regenerative Landscapes— Remediating Places
Fig. 1: © Christa Panick
Figs. 2–7: © Michael Latz

Studio 804
Figs. 1–7: Courtesy Studio 804.

Dongtan Eco City
Figs. 1–2: © Arup

Toward an Ecological Building Envelope: Research, Design, and Innovation
Fig. 1: © Hallkin Photography LLC
Fig. 2: © Elliot Kaufman
Fig. 4: © KieranTimberlake

Material Ecologies in Architecture
Fig. 1: Courtesy Solar Electric Light Fund. Fig. 2: Courtesy Parans. Fig. 3: Courtesy Toyota Motor Corporation, Japan.
Fig. 4: Photo by Antal Szentendrei, courtesy of Litracon. Fig. 5: Courtesy Italcementi Archives. Figs. 6–7: Drawing by Stephen Gage and Will Thorne. Figs. 8–9: Courtesy Stephen Gage and Will Thorne.

Toward a Productive Excess
Fig. 1: Courtesy of Charles E. Young Library, Department of Special Collections, collection #344, "Expositions and Fairs Collection." Reproduced from: Burton Benedict, *The Anthropology of World's Fairs* (California: Scolar Press, 983), 94. Fig. 2: Reproduced from: Esther da Costa Meyer, *The Work of Antonio Sant'Elia* (New Haven: Yale University, 1995), plate 16. Figs. 4–5: Courtesy Greg Taylor, Lauren Taylor White, and Rachel Glabe Taylor of Studio Formwork. Figs. 6–7: Courtesy Olympic Delivery Authority. Fig. 8: Courtesy National Museum of Singapore and The Electric Canvas.

Front cover
Reproduced from György Kepes, ed., *Arts of the Environment* (Henley, UK: Aidan Ellis, 1972), 192–93. Permission courtesy Juan Navarro Baldeweg.

Back cover
Courtesy Gross.Max.

Published by
Princeton Architectural Press
37 East Seventh Street
New York, New York 10003

For a free catalog of books, call 1-800-722-6657.
Visit our website at www.papress.com.

Editor: Wendy Fuller
Design: Paul Wagner and Bree Anne Apperley

Special thanks to: Nettie Aljian, Sara Bader,
Nicola Bednarek, Janet Behning, Becca Casbon,
Carina Cha, Penny (Yuen Pik) Chu, Carolyn Deuschle,
Russell Fernandez, Pete Fitzpatrick, Jan Haux,
Clare Jacobson, Aileen Kwun, Nancy Eklund Later,
Linda Lee, Laurie Manfra, John Myers,
Katharine Myers, Dan Simon, Andrew Stepanian,
Jennifer Thompson, Joseph Weston, and
Deb Wood of Princeton Architectural Press
—Kevin C. Lippert, publisher

Library of Congress Cataloging-in-Publication Data

Design ecologies : essays on the nature of design /
Lisa Tilder and Beth Blostein, editors ; contributors,
Jane Amidon ... [et al.]. — 1st ed.
      p.   cm.
ISBN 978-1-56898-783-5 (alk. paper)
1. Design—Environmental aspects. 2. Sustainable
architecture. I. Tilder, Lisa, 1968- II. Blostein, Beth,
1968- III. Amidon, Jane. IV. Title.

NK1520.D465 2009
720'.47—dc22

2009012893